More Bloopers—Town Bonanzas!
The Baseball Hall of Shame™ 4

Q. Why was Joe Dugan of the 1927 New York Yankees fined $50—for hitting a single?
> (see chapter on *Batty Batters*)

Q. In a 1912 spring training game, an outfielder literally popped out of the gound to catch a fly ball. This comical rookie went on to be a veteran player and a Hall of Fame manager. Who was he?
> (see chapter on *The Blights of Spring*)

Q. Why did Minnesota Twins fans pelt Oakland A's manager Billy Martin with hundreds of marshmallows?
> (see chapter on *Booing the Boo Birds*)

Q. After whacking a home run over the fence, why did outfielder Frenchy Bordagaray slide into all four bases in a 1935 Dodgers-Giants game?
> (see chapter on *Corny Flakes*)

Q. Who—or what—was New York Met Kevin Elster's unlikely lunch date during the 1988 season?
> (see chapter on *Super-Silly Superstitions*)

THE BASEBALL HALL OF SHAME™ 4

BRUCE NASH AND ALLAN ZULLO

BERNIE WARD, CURATOR

POCKET BOOKS

New York   London   Toronto   Sydney   Tokyo   Singapore

An *Original* Publication of POCKET BOOKS

POCKET BOOKS, a division of Simon & Schuster
1230 Avenue of the Americas, New York, NY 10020

Nash, Bruce M.
    The Baseball Hall of Shame 4 / Bruce Nash and Allan Zullo.
        p. cm.
    ISBN: 0-671-74609-X
    1. Baseball—United States—Humor. 2. Baseball—United States—
Anecdotes. I. Zullo, Allan. II. Title.
GV863.A1N364   1990
796.357'0973—dc20   89-49629
                                                              CIP

First Pocket Books trade paperback printing April 1990

10 9 8 7 6 5 4 3 2

THE BASEBALL HALL OF SHAME is a trademark of
Nash and Zullo Productions, Inc.

POCKET and colophon are registered trademarks of
Simon & Schuster

Printed in the U.S.A.

In loving memory of Jim Graham, who was my ideal of what a good father and a good husband should be.

—B.N.

To Tom and Anna Wartowski, whose friendship means more to me than even a world championship for the Chicago Cubs.

—A.Z.

ACKNOWLEDGMENTS

We wish to thank all the fans, players, coaches, and sportswriters who contributed nominations.

We are especially grateful to those players, past and present, who shared a few laughs with us as they recounted the inglorious moments that earned them a place in The Baseball Hall of SHAME.

This book couldn't have been completed without the assistance and cooperation of the staff of the National Baseball Hall of Fame Library in Cooperstown, New York. We appreciate the help, guidance, and friendship of head librarian Tom Heitz and the outstanding research provided by senior research associate Bill Deane and assistant researchers Paul Cunningham and William Vaules.

We wish to acknowledge the outstanding efforts of Bill Althaus, Barbara Arnold, Ann Bauleke, Bill Borst, Colin Cameron, Ron Cook, Mike Imrem, Mike Paolercio, and Casey Tefertiller.

We also extend our thanks to Jeff Fritsch, Gary Hernbroth, Dick Larson, Kerry Loomis, and Scott Winslow.

And a very special thanks goes to the two greatest stars in our lineup, Sophie Nash and Kathy Zullo.

CONTENTS

LEADING OFF

There is no end to shame.

By 1987 we had crammed more than 100 years of baseball foul-ups into three volumes of *The Baseball Hall of SHAME*. But we soon realized there were even more incredible, hilarious stories that had yet to be chronicled. It was only a matter of time before we returned with our fourth shameful volume on baseball.

After all, our national pastime provides us with a never-ending supply of embarrassingly funny moments. Just in the last few years alone, players such as Bo Jackson, Vince Coleman, Tony Gwynn, Bret Saberhagen, Kirk Gibson, and Wade Boggs have made rib-tickling boners that earned them enshrinement in Blooperstown. Among the new inductees is the Milwaukee Brewers' Terry Francona, who was ejected from a game after receiving an intentional walk. Terry is the younger half of The Baseball Hall of SHAME's first father-and-son inductees. His dad, Tito Francona of the Cleveland Indians, made it into *The Baseball Hall of SHAME 3* for sneakily tricking the opposing pitcher into committing a game-losing balk.

Since our third volume was published, we have received hundreds of nominations from readers and from fans whom we met on our cross-country travels to major league ball parks. From the dugouts and clubhouses, players and coaches tipped us off to other great stories of unforgettable blunders. Many more incidents of ignobility surfaced when we spent days digging through the archives at the National Baseball Hall of Fame and Museum in Cooperstown, New York.

Among those fondly dishonored in *The Baseball Hall of SHAME 4* are such Hall of Famers as Mickey Mantle and Dizzy Dean, as well as such wacky characters from the early days of baseball as "Eagle Eye" Beckley, Bugs Raymond, Jumping Joe Dugan, and Daredevil Dave Altizer.

The grand old game will continue to produce more hilarious happenings on and off the field. And we will continue to chronicle these embarrassing moments of both the superstars and the bozos. As we've always said, "Fame *and* shame are part of the game."

HOLEY MITTS!

◆

You can tell who they are in the box score by their first initial—E. They are the fabulous fumblers who somehow make it to the bigs with holes in their gloves. These fielders have only one weakness— batted balls. They boot so many balls, they belong on a soccer field, not a baseball diamond. For "The Most Inept Fielding Perfor- mances," The Baseball Hall of SHAME inducts the following:

Bob Uecker

Catcher • Atlanta, N.L. • Sept. 7, 1967

Bob Uecker—"Mr. Baseball" himself—holds the dubious dishonor of suffer- ing the worst day ever for a catcher.

Before he was finally yanked from the lineup in the seventh inning, Bumbling Bob was charged with catcher's interference, a throwing error, and two passed balls—including one that allowed the winning run to score.

Halfway through the 1967 season the Atlanta Braves—for reasons that defy explanation—traded veteran catcher Gene Oliver to the Philadelphia Phillies in exchange for Uecker, who was batting all of .171 at the time.

This was the player who once shagged fly balls in the outfield with a tuba. This was the player who said the highlight of his career was walking with the bases loaded to drive in the winning run in an intrasquad game in spring training. This was the player who claimed the Phillies once honored him with a Bob Uecker Day Off.

Uecker, whose lack of baseball skills made everyone else on the club— including the batboy—look great, was the backup catcher who was supposed to handle the fluttering pitches of knuckleballer Phil Niekro. "The way to catch a knuckleball is to wait until the ball stops rolling and then pick it up," Uecker once said.

People assumed he was joking. But on that fateful night in Pittsburgh in 1967, it looked like he was serious.

Bob experienced everything bad that could happen to a catcher. He first gained the notice of the fans in the fourth inning when he was called for catcher's interference. His glove got in the way of batter Maury Wills's swing, so Wills was awarded first base.

"Bob was sitting up as close to the hitter as he could get to catch the knuckleball before it broke," recalled Braves manager Billy Hitchcock. "Uecker kept crowding up closer and closer under the hitters, until he finally got called on it."

But the fourth inning was only a preview of the disaster that awaited Bob in the next frame.

With Roberto Clemente on second base, Willie Stargell struck out. But Uecker let the third strike get by him for a passed ball. Clemente dashed to third while Bob chased down the ball. He managed to throw out Stargell only because Willie was one of the decade's slowest runners.

Niekro struck out the next batter, Donn Clendenon, but Uecker was guilty of another passed ball. Only this time, Clemente scored what turned out to be the winning run and Clendenon made it safely to first.

Bob's woes weren't over yet. The next hitter, Gene Alley, forced Clendenon at second. Then on the following pitch, Alley tried to steal second. Uecker leaped out of his crouch and threw a strike—to Mack Jones in center field, for an error. Alley continued to third on Bob's wild throw and scored moments later on a hit.

In the seventh inning Hitchcock ordered the injured Joe Torre to pinch-hit for Uecker, who had gone hitless in two previous trips. Torre doubled and later scored, but the Braves lost 4–2, thanks in large part to Uecker.

"I finally had to get Uecker out of there, even though Torre was hurt," said Hitchcock. "I figured Bob had done just about everything wrong a catcher could do. And I was afraid that if I left him in there any longer, he'd invent a few more bad things."

New York Mets

Aug. 27, 1963

The early New York Mets conjured up ways to lose that no one knew existed. But no defeat was goofier than their 1963 last-inning fielding fiasco against the Pittsburgh Pirates.

A dumbfounded *New York Times* reporter who witnessed the debacle wrote, "Even to those who may be inured by exposure to the ability of the New York Mets to fritter away a ball game at the last moment, tonight's 2–1 loss to the Pittsburgh Pirates is hard to describe and harder to believe."

The Mets clung to a 1–0 lead going into the bottom of the ninth in Pittsburgh. For a brief moment, the Mets looked like contenders instead of pretenders. But it was just an illusion.

Pitcher Galen Cisco got the first man out in the ninth, but walked Dick Schofield. The next batter, Manny Mota, slapped a little grounder back up the middle. On any other team and at any other time, it would have been a routine, game-ending double play. But these were the Mets.

The bouncing ball skipped past Cisco's outstretched fingertips. Second baseman Ron Hunt and shortstop Al Moran cut across the infield to head it off at the pass, but after almost colliding, they watched it bound into the outfield.

Center fielder Duke Carmel was the next Met to get a shot at stopping the ball. In keeping with tradition, Duke charged the ball only to watch in dismay as it bounced over his glove for an error.

Right fielder Joe Christopher, who had just been inserted into the lineup for his defensive skills, backed up the play. Christopher finally corralled the ball and then heaved a mighty peg—somewhere into the vast, uncharted region between third base and home—for another error. Cisco tried to run down the wild throw in foul territory, but he tripped and fell flat on his face.

Meanwhile, Schofield had rounded third and was heading for home with Mota chugging past second. As Cisco scrambled to his feet, Schofield scored the tying run. By the time Cisco had chased down the ball at the backstop, Mota was barreling toward home with the winning run.

There was still a last-gasp chance for heroics. Cisco fired the ball to catcher Jesse Gonder in plenty of time to nail Mota. However, Gonder stood with his back to the plate to take Cisco's throw. When he caught the ball, Gonder whirled around to make the tag. It was then that Gonder discovered he was a good five feet from home plate—too far away to tag Mota, who was now safely sliding across home with the winning run.

While the Pirates jumped for joy, Mets manager Casey Stengel flew into a rage. Infuriated over the incredible comedy of errors, Stengel stood on the dugout steps, ripped off his cap, and flung it at his fumbling fielders.

Pointing to his cap, Stengel shouted at them, "Let's see if you can pick *that* up!"

Kirk Gibson

Right Fielder • Detroit, A.L. • April 9, 1981

In his most mortifying game ever, All-Star outfielder Kirk Gibson got bonked on the head *twice* with fly balls.

And it happened on, of all days, Opening Day in front of a packed stadium of unforgiving hometown fans.

Throughout spring training in 1981, the Detroit Tigers' 23-year-old outfielder had been working out in left and center field in preparation for the coming season.

"I was really looking forward to Opening Day," Gibson recalled. "It's like a holiday in Detroit. Everybody takes off work and goes to the game. You can't get another person in the stadium, and everybody there expects the Tigers to win.

"I walked into the clubhouse, knowing I was going to start in my first Opening Day game. I figured I would be playing either left or center field. When I looked at the lineup card, I couldn't believe it. There was a 'nine' beside my name. I had to play right field.

" 'Oh, God,' I thought. 'It's an afternoon game, there's not a cloud in the sky, and Tiger Stadium is one of the worst places in the early spring to play right field in the day.' I went to [manager] Sparky Anderson and said, 'I think you've made a mistake in the lineup.' And Sparky said, 'No, I didn't. I know you can play right field.' Having the big ego that I do, I said, 'Sure I can.' "

But it just wasn't Gibson's day in the sun.

The first ball hit to him was misplayed off his head in the second inning

on a deep fly ball hit by the Toronto Blue Jays' Willie Upshaw. "I kept going back, back, back until I was against the wall," Gibson recalled. "I lost it in the sun, and the ball whacked right off the side of my head and bounced back toward the infield. I was so embarrassed. I began to hear some boos."

In the next inning, with Lloyd Moseby on third base, John Mayberry hit a soft shallow line drive to right. Gibson broke late, then charged the ball and caught it right off his shoe tops. But although he was in shallow right, he couldn't stop Moseby from tagging up at third and scoring because he had dropped the ball after the catch.

"They really started to boo me—even when I came up to bat," Gibson recalled. "When I returned to the outfield, I kept thinking, 'Oh, man, don't hit another one out here to me.' Sure enough, here comes another one."

In the fifth inning Ernie Whitt hit a high fly ball to right. Gibson didn't drift in toward the ball; he staggered in. Squeamish fans in the stands turned their heads away, not wanting to see how he'd butcher the play.

"The ball was right dead in the middle of the sun, and I wasn't real good at using my glasses at the time," said Gibson. "But I had my glasses down and I saw it, and then I thought I saw it, and then I didn't. The next thing I knew it bounced off my right ear and he [Whitt] ended up on third. I got booed unmercifully by 51,000 people, and I felt so humiliated. I'd never been booed like that in my whole life."

After the game, which Detroit won 6–2, Gibson told reporters, "I had some tough times, but we won anyway. I'll learn from my mistakes. I'll improve. I fielded that last single without any trouble. See, I'm getting better already."

Everything Under the Sun

In a 1913 game, St. Louis Cardinals right fielder Steve Evans lost two fly balls in the sun.

The embarrassed Evans didn't want to suffer any more gaffes. So he sauntered over to the bleachers, snatched a Japanese parasol from a startled fan, and took it back with him to his position in right field. For the rest of the inning, Evans played under the parasol.

Jake "Eagle Eye" Beckley

First Baseman • Pittsburgh–New York–Cincinnati–St. Louis, N.L. 1888–1907

At the plate, Hall of Famer Jake Beckley had the eye of an eagle. But on the field, he had the arm of a monkey.

He could hit pitches better than most anyone—he owned a .308 lifetime batting average—but he couldn't throw worth a damn. Such a glaring fault did not go unnoticed by the opposition. They ran wild whenever Beckley had the ball.

Tommy Leach of the Pittsburgh Pirates never failed to take advantage of Jake's scattergun arm. During a 1905 game when Beckley was playing first base for the St. Louis Cardinals, Leach laid down a bunt that required Jake to field the ball. Pitcher Jack Taylor hurried to cover the bag on the play. Beckley scooped up the ball and, rather than risk a bad throw with an overhand motion, tossed the ball underhanded. It sailed three feet over Taylor's head.

Leach motored around first and headed for second. Jake, wanting to redeem himself, dashed past Taylor and recovered the ball. By now Leach was running full bore for third. When he noticed that Beckley had the ball, Leach, with no regard at all for Jake's arm, scampered for home.

Instead of taking a chance on throwing the ball, Beckley decided to sprint for the plate. After a mad dash, he dove headfirst for the plate and tagged Leach in the ribs as the runner slid in feet first. When the dust settled, Leach was out at home and out of the game—with two broken ribs.

Beckley made up for his throwing shortcomings by pulling off the old hidden ball trick. He often hid the ball under the base when the runner wasn't looking. Then, whenever the runner took a lead-off, Beckley would pull the ball out and tag him. But one time it backfired badly.

In a 1906 game, Pirates runner Honus Wagner was on first when Jake sneakily hid the ball under the base. When Wagner took his lead-off, Beckley slyly reached down for the ball, but he couldn't find it. Seeing this, Wagner took off for second. Jake had forgotten under which corner he had hid the ball! Frantically, he lifted each corner of the base until he found it. Then he made a hurried and, as usual, wild throw to second, allowing Wagner to reach third.

Then there was the time in 1903 when Beckley, playing first for the Cincinnati Reds, tried a new twist to the hidden ball trick. After Pirates runner Otto Krueger had beaten out a bunt, Jake pretended to throw the ball back to pitcher Noodles Hahn. But Beckley had slipped the ball up his own sleeve. Krueger, unaware of the chicanery, edged off the bag. Beckley reached up his sleeve to snatch the ball, but couldn't pull it out. After watching the flustered Reds first sacker, Krueger figured out the scam and hightailed it for second. Meanwhile, Noodles Hahn raced over to Beckley and ripped the sleeve from his shirt and the ball dropped to the ground. Never again did Beckley have anything up his sleeve.

Tommy John

Pitcher • New York, A.L. • July 27, 1988

Tommy John made not one, not two, but *three* errors on one play!

"I've made errors before," said the veteran lefty, "but these seemed like a lifetime's worth in one play."

In a game against the Milwaukee Brewers, John's control on the mound was masterful. But in the field he fell apart at the seams like a dime-store baseball, and tied a dubious record that hadn't been equaled in 90 years.

With one out in the fourth inning and the New York Yankees ahead 4–0, John walked Jim Gantner. The next batter, Jeffrey Leonard, tapped a little dribbler to the left of the mound that John should have easily fielded for a routine out. But John bobbled the ball for error No. 1.

Gantner had already reached second and Leonard was almost at first when John—a pitcher who built his career on pinpoint control—reared back and heaved the ball past first baseman Don Mattingly and into right field. Error No. 2.

UPI/Bettmann Newsphotos

Gantner raced to third and was quickly waved home on the overthrow while Leonard galloped to second. The throw in from right fielder Dave Winfield was on line to cut down Gantner at the plate—but John unthinkingly cut off the relay. If mental blunders were officially recorded, this would have been another error on the play. As it was, John guaranteed himself a place in history when he whirled and threw a perfect strike into the Brewers dugout to complete a trifecta of gaffes. Gantner scored, and Leonard, who had reached third in a stroll, was waved home for the second run.

The embarrassed pitcher, who had rushed to cover home after his third miscue, muttered to plate umpire Richie Garcia, "I think I just lost a Gold Glove on that play."

It was the most deplorable fielding performance by a pitcher since a triple bungle by J. Bentley Seymour of the New York Giants in 1898. What made John's so shameful was that he made three errors on one play; Seymour needed a whole inning to rack up three miscues.

When the 45-year-old John—the oldest player in the majors in 1988—learned he had tied Seymour's record, he said, "I think I pitched against him in the Eastern League."

Reliving the ignoble incident, John said, "My instinct was to go after the grounder with two hands, but I didn't think I had enough time. I should have eaten it, but I thought I could get him [Leonard] with a good throw to first. Instead, I threw it into right field. That was my second mistake. Then I cut the ball off. That was another mistake. Then, I threw the ball to their trainer in the dugout.

"I do that every once in a while to get the team loose."

John, who won the game 16–3, thought he had an explanation for the blunders. "There was a thunderstorm coming and there were a lot of negative ions in the air and, since I was wearing a metal cup, it just glitched my mind."

Another Fine Mess

Pittsburgh Pirates right fielder Ray Rohwer had misplayed two fly balls and dropped another in a 1922 game, prompting anguished manager Bill McKechnie to mutter, "If I only had someone who could play out there."

Infielder Cotton Tierney eagerly spoke up: "I'm your man, Mr. McKechnie."

So the skipper sent Cotton out to right field. He played an easy fly ball for a triple. When Tierney returned to the dugout after the side had been retired, he told McKechnie, "Don't blame me for that play. Rohwer certainly put right field in a mess."

Eddie Joost

Shortstop • Philadelphia, A.L. • Sept. 11, 1948

In one of the wackiest fielding plays in major league history, Eddie Joost lost a ground ball in his shirt!

"It was definitely the most embarrassing moment of my life," admitted Joost, a big league infielder for 17 years. "There wasn't any place for me to hide out there. And the worst of it was that Ted Williams was laughing his head off at me. I looked like a real dunce."

Joost suffered his most mortifying moment while playing shortstop for the Philadelphia Athletics in a 1948 game against the Boston Red Sox at Fenway Park. In the bottom of the fourth inning, Williams was at second base with Billy Goodman at the plate.

Goodman rapped a sharp hopper past A's pitcher Bill McCahan, and Joost raced over to make the play. He bent down for the ball—but came up empty-handed. The ball had disappeared! "Nobody could figure out what had happened," Joost recalled. "McCahan was waiting for me to make the throw to first. When he didn't see anything happening, he ran over to me, waving his arms and yelling, 'Where in the hell did it go?'"

It took a few seconds for Joost to find the answer. Incredibly, the ball had bounced off the heel of his glove, rolled up his sleeve, and ended up in the back of his shirt.

Meanwhile, Goodman had made it safely to first and was credited with a hit, while Williams had reached third. The two runners, along with all the other players and fans in the stands, then cast their eyes on Joost as he tried frantically to retrieve the ball from his jersey.

Joost danced up and down like a man with an army of ants in his shirt. He scratched and clawed at his back, but the ball was still just a fingernail out of reach. In desperation, he began unbuttoning his jersey, but that was too slow, so he ripped the shirttail out of his pants. Finally, the ball fell to the ground.

The entire park erupted in laughter. Williams, who could have easily scored from third during Joost's wild search for the ball, had doubled over with laughter and was too weak to run.

"I picked up the ball and ran over to third base," Joost recalled. "I shook the ball in Ted's face and yelled at him, 'Okay, damn you! You can run now.'

"But he was laughing so hard he couldn't have run if he wanted to. Everybody was laughing—even me.

"You know, that never would have happened if we had worn those nice-fitting double-knits that they wear today."

Cross Rhodes

As a backup player for the New York Giants, Dusty Rhodes was a fine hitter but a lousy outfielder.

During a 1955 game, manager Leo Durocher sent Dusty out to play right field. One pitch later, Rhodes waved his arms, called time-out, and started for the dugout.

"Do you want your sunglasses?" Durocher asked.

"No," replied Rhodes. "I want my helmet."

Richie Ashburn
Center Fielder

Frank Thomas
Left Fielder

Elio Chacon
Shortstop

New York, N.L. • May 1, 1962

When the 1962 New York Mets were dealt the cards of life, fate slipped in a few jokers. Things just never worked out the way the Mets had planned.

Take, for example, Richie Ashburn's desperate attempt to save his hide from collisions in the outfield.

Closing out a great career with the worst team in modern history, the veteran center fielder often dodged disaster in the form of energetic but modestly talented shortstop Elio Chacon. While chasing short fly balls, the two often came perilously close to crashing into each other.

"Elio was always running into people," Ashburn recalled. "He never actually hit me, but he came so close often enough, that I knew it would just be a matter of time before he nailed me. Every time I went after a short fly, I had to keep one eye on the ball and one on Elio."

The problem was, they weren't communicating. In fact, they weren't even speaking the same language. Chacon, a native of Caracas, Venezuela, spoke no English. And Ashburn, a native of Tilden, Nebraska, spoke no Spanish. Whenever Ashburn ran in on a short fly, he yelled, "I got it! I got it!" Meanwhile, Chacon was dashing out, shouting the same thing in Spanish, so that the Mets sounded like they were baseball's version of the Tower of Babel.

Ashburn feared he'd never make it through that dismal season and ease gracefully into retirement without being maimed for life. So he took his worries to Joe Christopher, his fellow outfielder who spoke both English and Spanish.

"Instead of calling 'I got it' in English, say it in Spanish," suggested Christopher. "Just shout, *'Yo lo tengo.'* Elio will understand you. I'll explain it to Elio so he knows what's going on."

A relieved Ashburn spent the rest of the day practicing his Spanish until he had the phrase down pat. Just before game time, he approached Elio. *"Yo lo tengo?"* he asked.

"Sí, sí!" replied a beaming Chacon. *"Yo lo tengo!"*

But the carefully laid plan unraveled a few hours later during a game against the Cincinnati Reds. With the bases loaded, the Reds' Frank Robinson lofted a short fly ball to shallow left-center field.

Ashburn sprinted in for the catch, yelling at the top of his voice, *"Yo lo tengo! Yo lo tengo!"* Chacon, who had scampered after the ball, pulled up and happily motioned for Ashburn to take it.

Ashburn, convinced his problem was finally solved, reached out to make the easy catch—and was flattened by six-foot, three-inch, 200-pound Frank Thomas, the Mets' hard-charging left fielder. Thomas spoke no Spanish.

BATTY BATTERS

◆

A hitter's greatest fear is not necessarily going zero-for-July or possessing an average that would embarrass a bowler. No, his worst fear is looking bad at the plate. Some of the game's best-known players have taken their turn at bat and returned to the dugout without a shred of dignity. For "The Most Pitiful Appearances at the Plate," The Baseball Hall of SHAME inducts the following:

Bo Jackson

Right Fielder • Kansas City, A.L. • Sept. 17, 1986

When Bo Jackson first came up to the majors at the end of the 1986 season, he wasn't nearly the threat as a batter as he was as college football's best player.

In 25 games for the Kansas City Royals, the former Auburn star and Heisman Trophy winner struck out 34 times and batted only .207. It was obvious he needed to learn to hit the curveball, to study the strike zone— and to know the difference between a walk and a balk.

It was that last item that caused him the most embarrassment so far in his major league career.

In the seventh inning of a game against the California Angels in Anaheim, Jackson was facing 300-game winner Don Sutton with a runner on first. Bo immediately got himself into a hole, whiffing on the first two pitches. Then he took a ball.

On the 1-and-2 pitch, Sutton failed to come to a complete stop on his delivery and plate umpire Jim Evans immediately shouted, "Balk!"

To everyone's surprise, Jackson dropped his bat and began trotting down to first base. "Don't ask me why, but I got a balk confused with a walk," Bo sheepishly recalled. "When the umpire called 'balk,' I thought he said 'walk,' and I headed down toward first base."

First base umpire Durwood Merrill stopped Jackson and reminded him that the count was only 2-and-2 and that it would be best for all concerned if he would kindly return to the batter's box. "Boy, was that embarrassing," said Bo. "If I could have disappeared, I would have, believe me."

As Jackson returned to the batter's box, the bench jockeys—even those on his own team—went into overdrive.

"Guys were rolling around on the bench, they were laughing so hard," recalled Royals infielder Buddy Biancalana. "The guys got on him pretty good after that play."

Said Kansas City manager John Wathan, "I thought we were going to have to send Bo back to Auburn and make him take his math classes over again."

Bo's premature walk may have shown him to be psychic, because two pitches later he walked—this time on ball four.

Cookie Cuccurullo

Pitcher • Pittsburgh, N.L. • Aug. 15, 1945

No batter was more jittery at the plate than Cookie Cuccurullo, especially the day when he was called on to pinch-hit with the game on the line.

Cookie was a high-strung southpaw relief pitcher who won only three games in his three years in the majors. He simply couldn't handle stress very well, so he usually pitched only in the early innings. However, Cookie was a decent batter who sometimes pinch-hit.

But the tense young player was never used in a clutch situation—except for a flustered appearance during a 1945 game between the Pittsburgh Pirates and the New York Giants.

The Pirates trailed 9–7 in the ninth inning when Frankie Gustine and Al Lopez both singled. With the tying runs on base, pitcher Rip Sewell, a .286 hitter, was due up. But to everyone's surprise, manager Frankie Frisch sat him down.

Staring down at the end of the bench, the manager hollered, "Cookie, get a bat and go up and pinch-hit."

Cuccurullo, suffering a sudden attack of cold shivers, didn't move. He couldn't believe his ears.

"Cookie!" shouted Frisch again. "Get going!"

His heart pounding in fear, Cuccurullo nervously grabbed a bat and nearly stumbled as he climbed the dugout steps. By the time he reached the batter's box, Cookie was trembling so badly he could hardly hold the bat. Fortunately for him, he didn't have to hold it for long.

The first pitch from Giants pitcher Harry Feldman was a big looping curveball that broke low and inside. Cookie quickly skipped out of the way.

The ball just missed his foot and glanced off catcher Ernie Lombardi's mitt. The ball took a crazy bounce to the backstop and caromed toward the Giants dugout along the third base line.

As soon as the ball got by the catcher, everybody started running: Lombardi from behind the plate, Gustine from second base, Lopez from first.

And Cuccurullo from home.

Since everybody else was running, the nervous Nellie got so flustered, he dropped his bat and took off running too!

While Lombardi—the slowest man in baseball—lumbered after the elusive ball, Gustine and Lopez scampered around the bases. Since no Giant bothered to cover home, both Pirates scored to tie the game. Cookie, meanwhile, finished his frantic dash with a dramatic slide into third.

When Lombardi retrieved the ball, he rambled back to home plate and complained to umpire Beans Reardon that the ball had actually hit Cuccurullo in the foot. If so, that would mean Lopez and Gustine would have to go back to second and third and Cookie would go to first.

But Reardon insisted that the ball had not hit the batter. Lombardi had barely started to jaw with Reardon before player-manager Mel Ott joined the fracas. "The ball hit him!" Ott shouted.

"No, it didn't!" Reardon yelled back.

"Well, if the ball didn't hit him, what's he doing down there?" Ott demanded, pointing to Cookie at third base.

Reardon did a classic double-take and said, "What's who doing where?" Realizing that the runner was Cookie, the ump told Ott, "I thought that was Lopez."

With a small army of Giants at his heels, Reardon strode to third and confronted Cookie. "What the hell are you doing here?" Reardon thundered. "Why did you run?"

"I—I don't know," stammered Cuccurullo. "I—I just saw everybody else running, and I got so excited, I ran too."

"Well, you can't do that," roared the ump. "Now get back there and hit."

Cookie never got the chance. Frisch immediately yanked him for another pinch hitter and never called on Cuccurullo to bat again with the game on the line.

Thinking of a Strikeout

On or off the field, Yogi Berra unwittingly made people laugh.

In 1950, New York Yankees manager Casey Stengel tried to help the catcher break his bad habit of swinging at pitches out of the strike zone.

"Wait out the pitcher," Stengel told him. "Concentrate on the strike zone, think about what he's going to throw you, and don't give him any help."

On his next trip to the plate, Yogi waited the pitcher out—for three fast strikes that blazed across the plate. When Berra returned to the bench, he complained to Stengel, "How in the hell can you think and hit at the same time?"

Ron "Rocky" Swoboda

Outfielder • New York, N.L. • June 22, 1969

Ron Swoboda received a standing ovation after tying a major league batting record. Unfortunately, the mark he tied was for striking out five consecutive times in one game, and the ovation he got came from his very own fans!

"I didn't want to strike out," Swoboda recalled. "But if I didn't, the fans would have felt cheated. It was against my nature, my training, my instincts to strike out. But when I walked up to home plate, it was on my mind, as it was on everybody else's."

More than 55,000 New York Mets fans who had jammed into Shea Stadium witnessed ignominious history being made. In the first inning, with two on and two out, Swoboda struck out swinging. The fans had seen this happen all too often before, so, as they had done so many times that year, they booed Rocky lustily.

The booing grew louder in the third inning when Swoboda took a called third strike with two on. And the booing was deafening when he fanned to end the fourth inning, again with two on. Swoboda kept his horrendous streak intact when he led off the seventh inning by whiffing.

The fans realized they just might see something really historic, if only Rocky could get up to bat again. But the next inning, the bottom of the eighth, appeared to be the Mets' last chance at bat, since they were beating the St. Louis Cardinals 5–1 and Swoboda was the sixth hitter due up.

Two walks and two outs later, Donn Clendenon stepped to the plate with Swoboda on deck. The fans clamored for Clendenon to get on base so Rocky would have a final shot at the record. When a wild pitch opened first base, Clendenon was walked intentionally, and the stadium rocked with cheers as Swoboda stepped to the plate.

Rocky now faced the daunting challenge of striking out five consecutive times in one game—a dubious feat that up until then only 12 men in 100 years of baseball had ever done in a nine-inning game.

As Rocky stepped into the batter's box, he whispered to catcher Tim McCarver, "Do you think I've got a chance for five in a row?"

"The way you're swinging today," said McCarver, "you've got a hell of a chance."

The first pitch from Cardinals reliever Ron Willis was a strike, and the fans responded with glee. Whistling and clapping, they waved their fists and encouraged their antihero.

Recalled Rocky, "I told myself, I owe it to the fans to strike out. If I don't strike out, they will think I let them down."

The fans booed when the next pitch was called a ball. They didn't want Swoboda to be denied his place in history by getting a walk. Rocky fouled off the next offering. Now the crowd went wild because their anguished Met was down to his last strike—just one futile swing away from ignobility.

"I knew if I struck out five times, I deserved to be booed," he recalled. "I deserved to be booed in the clubhouse, I deserved to be booed driving home, and I deserved to be booed when I walked in the front door."

As the fans held their breath, the 1–2 pitch cut the outside corner of the plate. Swoboda swung feebly—and missed the ball by a foot. If there was any booing, it was drowned out by an incredible roar. In unison, 55,000 fans leaped to their feet in a standing ovation and yelled themselves hoarse as their embarrassed whiffing wonder dropped his bat at home plate and, with his head low, walked slowly to his outfield position.

"When I struck out the first time, I figured I'd get him the next time," Rocky told reporters after the game, which the Mets won 5–1. "When I struck out the second time, I wondered what was going on. The third time, it seemed funny that I couldn't connect. The fourth time, it was just a big bad joke. Now, the fifth time, it was history.

"I guess if we had lost the game, I would have been eating my heart out. As it is, I'm only eating out one ventricle."

Len Koenecke

Outfielder • Brooklyn, N.L. • Aug. 31, 1934

In one of the most shameful cases of absentmindedness by a batter, Len Koenecke laid down a bunt—and then forgot to run!

Koenecke showed he could handle the bat in his first full season as a major leaguer. His .320 batting average and 14 home runs ranked tops among the Dodgers. Apparently, though, the young Dodger forgot how to handle a simple bunt.

He displayed his forgetfulness during the second inning of a game against the New York Giants. After Dodger batter Sam Leslie beat out a single, manager Casey Stengel flashed the bunt sign to Koenecke, who was the next hitter. Koenecke squared around to bunt and dumped the ball three feet in front of home plate. Giants catcher Gus Mancuso sprang out of his crouch like a cat and pounced on the ball.

Mancuso thought he had a chance to nail Leslie at second and fired the ball to shortstop Travis Jackson, who was covering the bag. But the ball sailed over his head as Leslie headed for third.

Meanwhile, back at home plate, Mancuso heard some loud cheering behind him. He turned around and, to his surprise, saw Koenecke standing at the plate, acting as excited over the play as any of the paying customers in the Ebbets Field box seats. Koenecke was jumping up and down, rooting for his Dodger teammate to make third on the overthrow.

Stengel couldn't believe his eyes. He charged out of the dugout screaming his head off at the forgetful Koenecke. "Go to first, you idiot! Go to first!" the manager shouted.

By this time, Giants center fielder Hank Leiber had run down the ball and heaved it to Johnny Vergez at third base. But Leslie beat the throw.

With the runner safe at third—and with Stengel raising a dust storm outside the dugout—Koenecke suddenly woke up and realized he was supposed to be running and not watching. He still had a bunt to beat out. So finally he took off for first. But Vergez threw him out by 60 feet. The only place left for the embarrassed Dodger to run was the dugout, where he got a tongue lashing from Stengel that he never forgot.

Singling Out the Culprit

The 1927 New York Yankees—considered by many the best team in baseball history—had standards for excellence that far exceeded those of any other team.

During the fifth inning of a spring training exhibition game against the Brooklyn Dodgers, the Yankee bats exploded. Earle Combs doubled to left and Mark Koenig doubled to right. Then Babe Ruth hit one out of the ball park. Next, Lou Gehrig tripled to center, Tony Lazzeri whaled a homer, and Bob Meusel belted a triple. Joe Dugan then dumped a puny Texas League single to center.

When Dugan returned to the dugout after scoring, manager Miller Huggins told him, "You're fined fifty bucks, Joe."

"Me? Why?" asked a stunned Dugan.

"Because your lousy single broke up a darn good rally."

José Nunez

Pitcher • Toronto, A.L. • March, 1988

José Nunez had one of baseball's sorriest and silliest at-bats.

During a 1988 spring training game with the Philadelphia Phillies in Clearwater, Florida, the Toronto Blue Jays were playing by National League rules. That meant they could not use a designated hitter. As a result, Nunez, the Toronto hurler, had to bat for the first time ever in his pro career. He hadn't even batted in the minors because those leagues had also used the DH.

Trying to look like a veteran hitter, Nunez stepped into the batter's box, waggled his bat menacingly, spit contemptuously, and waited for the pitch.

"Ah, José," said plate umpire Dave Pallone. "You still have your warm-up jacket on." Nunez retreated to the dugout, shed his jacket, and strode back to the plate.

"Ah, José," Pallone interrupted again. "About your batting helmet. You have the wrong one on." Nunez, swinging from the left side, wore a helmet for a right-handed hitter, with the earflap covering his left ear rather than his right ear.

To José, it was easy to fix. He simply turned the helmet around and wore it catcher style, with the bill of the cap in the back. That way, the flap was over the right ear.

But Pallone waved his arms and said, "No, no. You need to get a lefty's helmet."

But Nunez had already made one too many trips back to the dugout. So he simply walked across the plate and batted right-handed and straightened out his batting helmet.

By now both benches were convulsed with laughter. So were Pallone, Phillies pitcher Kevin Gross, and catcher Lance Parrish. After waiting for Nunez to get his act together, Gross looked in for the sign and then saw Nunez bent over, peering back at Parrish instead of facing the pitcher.

"What the hell are you doing?" Parrish demanded.

Nunez said matter-of-factly, "I want to see the signs."

Being a nice guy, Parrish said, "Okay, what pitch do you want?"

"Give me a fastball," said Nunez.

Parrish flashed the sign and Gross fired a fast ball which Nunez fouled off. Then José turned to Parrish again and changed his request. "Make the next one a change-up."

Pallone couldn't take it anymore. He called time and doubled over with laughter. It took a couple of minutes for Parrish, Gross, and Pallone to compose themselves. Finally the game resumed and, on a 2–2 pitch, Nunez grounded out.

Said a Blue Jays spokesman, "José did not, according to rumor, mistakenly grip the bat by the barrel the first time up. But no one would have been surprised if he had."

Shameful Moments in Batting

1988—After flying out to extend his hitless streak to 0-for-14, Philadelphia Phillies superstar Mike Schmidt passed San Diego Padres first baseman John Kruk and said, "Give me a gun. I'm ready to shoot myself in the head." Responded the smart-alecky Kruk: "Better not. You'll probably miss."

1987—Over the course of two games, each of which went into extra innings,

Eric Davis of the Cincinnati Reds became the only player in major league history to strike out a total of nine straight times.

1975—During a three-game series against the Boston Red Sox at Fenway Park, Milwaukee Brewers star Gorman Thomas (shown in photo) struck out eight straight times and hit into a double play—a pitiful performance that did not go unnoticed by the appreciative Boston fans. Recalled Thomas, "I got a standing ovation for hitting into the double play, and when I got out to center field, a dog ran out in front of me and relieved himself, and I got another standing ovation."

1954—Baltimore Orioles catcher Clint Courtney was at bat with a 3-and-2 count with two out in the bottom of the ninth when the umpires held up the game because of pouring rain. Two hours later they resumed play. After waiting all that time to finish his at-bat, Courtney stepped into the batter's box—and took the first pitch right down the heart of the plate for strike three to end the game.

RUN FOR YOUR LIVES!

◆

Some players are such horrendous runners they could use a second base coach. It's not that their legs are slow, but that their minds are working at only quarter speed. To others, running the base paths can be as foolish and reckless as strolling down a dark alley after midnight. For "The Most Absurd Baserunning Fiascoes," The Baseball Hall of SHAME inducts the following:

Gene Freese

Third Baseman • Pittsburgh, N.L. • May 28, 1955

The most infamous baserunning boner in baseball history was repeated nearly a half century later when Pittsburgh Pirates rookie Gene Freese forgot to touch second base.

The Pirates should have won 5–4, but lost instead because of his incredible gaffe.

Freese duplicated the classic blunder of New York Giants rookie Fred Merkle. In a game played Sept. 23, 1908, Merkle was running from first base after a teammate singled in what appeared to be the winning run in the bottom of the ninth inning. But Merkle forgot to touch second base and the run was disallowed. Because of the controversy that followed, the game was replayed. The Giants lost that game, and as a result lost the pennant to the Chicago Cubs.

"People called me Merkle after my boner," recalled Freese. "But, hell, he cost them the pennant. All I did was move my team from 31 games out of first place to 32."

Freese's baserunning bungle happened during a home game between the last-place Pirates and the Philadelphia Phillies. In the bottom of the tenth inning of a 4–4 deadlock, Pittsburgh had a chance to break out of a long losing streak. The Pirates had runners Tom Saffell on third and Freese on first with two out. Batter Ramon Mejias then punched a single to center that scored Saffell for what the Pirates thought was a much-needed 5–4 win. But it was not to be.

"I started toward second," Freese recounted. "But I was so happy to see we'd finally won a game after losing about ten straight that I turned around and went back to first to shake hands with Ramon. Then I ran to the dugout."

Phillies center fielder Richie Ashburn spotted the mental lapse and fired the ball to shortstop Roy Smalley, who touched second base for a force-out.

"My brother Bud, who was on the team, saw what happened," Freese said. "He came off the bench and tried to drag me back onto the field. I pulled away from him and ran into the clubhouse. But nobody followed me. I thought, 'Gee, that's a hell of a victory celebration.'"

The umpires, who had started walking off the field, were surrounded by angry Phillies claiming that the force-out at second had ended the inning and that the run was nullified. The umpires agreed and ordered the Pirates to take the field for the top of the 11th inning. But first the umps had to clear the diamond of hundreds of victory-starved fans who had swarmed onto the field, thinking the game was over.

Given a second chance, the Phillies tallied four quick runs to win 8–4.

"That was probably the shortest winning streak ever—a few minutes—but my whole career was like that," said Freese. "[Manager] Fred Haney jumped all over me and said that since I was a rookie, a boneheaded play like that would stick with me for the rest of my life. I told him I doubted it. You have to be good before people remember how bad you are."

What We Have Here Is a Failure to Communicate

The Washington Senators lost the fourth game of the 1933 World Series to the New York Giants because of a breakdown in communication.

With the score tied 1–1 in the bottom of the sixth inning, the Senators had Dave "Sheriff" Harris at second base with two outs. On a single to left field, third base coach Al Schacht waved Harris home and yelled, "Go! Go! Go!"

It looked like Harris would have scored easily, but he ran with his head down and stopped at third. When asked why he didn't streak for home, Harris told Schacht, "I thought you said 'whoa' instead of 'go.'" Harris didn't score in that inning and the Senators lost the game 2–1.

Ernie Lombardi

Catcher • Brooklyn-Cincinnati-Boston-New York, N.L. • 1931–47

In baseball the definition of slow has two words: Ernie Lombardi.

When the Hall of Fame catcher ran the bases, it was all uphill. His heart raced in overdrive but his feet were stuck in first gear. He simply couldn't run; he lumbered.

Lombardi—known by both players and fans as "The Schnozz" because of his Cyrano de Bergerac nose—had a ponderous, molasseslike stride. The six-foot, two-inch, 235-pound slowfoot lost countless doubles and triples because it took him so long just to reach first. His teammates used to needle him by saying, "Lombardi doubled to left field and beat out a single."

Incredibly, he was so slow that he once hit a ball off the left-field fence 330 feet away from home plate and was *still* thrown out at first! During a 1935 game against the visiting Chicago Cubs, Ernie drilled a shot that hit the top of the fence at Cincinnati's Crosley Field. Cubs left fielder Augie Galan grabbed the carom off the wall and fired the ball to shortstop Billy Jurges, whose relay to first beat the slowpoke by a step.

In spite of the fact that he ran the bases with the speed of an overloaded moving van with four flat tires, Lombardi led the National League in hitting in 1938 and 1942 and owned a lifetime batting average of .306. The only reasons why he didn't have an even higher average were that he never beat out infield squibblers and he was often thrown out at first on apparent singles to right field.

Because Ernie was such a ferocious hitter and ponderous runner, opposing third basemen and shortstops played him on the outfield grass. Lombardi once said that Brooklyn Dodgers shortstop Pee Wee Reese had been in the league four years before Lombardi realized he was an infielder.

The one time Ernie displayed any speed at all, it was deemed newsworthy enough to make headlines. *The New York World-Telegram* ran this account Sept. 6, 1946:

SCHNOZZ OUTRUNS (YES, OUTRUNS) CAP SNATCHER

At long last, Ernie Lombardi has won a foot race. The slowest man in baseball, irked when a 12-year-old filched his cap at the close of yesterday's game in the Polo Grounds, chased the youngster right out of the park and caught him near the subway entrance. But the cap was gone . . .

In his 17 seasons in the majors, Lombardi averaged one stolen base every two years. His blinding slowness seemed to paralyze the opposition. During a 1942 game against the Philadelphia Phillies, Ernie went chugging toward

second. The sight of this immense slowpoke attempting to steal sent shock waves through the Phils. Catcher Bennie Warren, holding the ball in his mitt, stared with his mouth agape before heaving the ball over the second baseman's head. Center fielder Ernie Koy—not believing it was possible for Lombardi to swipe a base—let the errant throw roll through his legs. Meanwhile, Schnozz rounded second, plodded to third, kept right on lumbering for home, and actually scored.

Lombardi's only steal in 1941 came against the Dodgers. He surprised everyone by taking off for second. Dodger catcher Mickey Owen instinctively drew back his arm to throw. But when he looked down to second, he saw the bag was vacant. Shortstop Pee Wee Reese and second baseman Billy Herman were so startled that neither one of them had covered the base, and Schnozz made it safely. Afterward, Brooklyn pitcher Kirby Higbe declared, "I could outrun Lombardi while carrying a mule on my back."

If Ernie wasn't kidded about his slowness, he was ribbed about his snoring. His nasal blasts could swing chandeliers and slam closet doors. As a result, he could never keep a roommate. "When Ernie snored, it sounded like he was about to die," recalled one former roomie. Don Brennan, who was the Schnozz's last roommate on the Reds, told the club he'd pay his own hotel expenses before staying in the same room with Lombardi again. A former roommate, Chick Hafey, tried to slip a clothespin over Lombardi's nose when he was snoring. But Hafey removed it when Ernie's face turned purple.

Allie Reynolds

Pitcher • New York, A.L. • April 19, 1948

After belting his first and only home run of his long career, Allie Reynolds had to be coaxed to circle the bases—because he refused to believe he had hit a round tripper.

The case of the bewildered base runner unfolded on Opening Day, 1948, at Griffith Stadium, the Washington Senators home park. What made it so mortifying was that Allie embarrassed himself in front of President Harry S Truman, Commissioner A. B. "Happy" Chandler, and a TV network audience. (The game was one of major league baseball's first telecasts.)

In the first inning the New York Yankees exploded for four quick runs and had two runners on base when Reynolds, the ninth man to bat in the frame, stepped to the plate. The Yankee pitching ace was hardly a threat with a bat. All he had to show for 13 years in the bigs was an anemic .163 lifetime batting average.

But on this day Allie teed off on an Early Wynn fastball and sent it soaring. Running toward first base with his head down, he never saw what everyone else in the ball park did—that the ball landed in the left-field bleachers.

"I hit it pretty hard, so I figured it was two bases for sure, and maybe three," Reynolds recalled. "I was the last person in the ball park who expected it to go over the fence. So when I rounded second base, I saw the third base coach with his arms up. It looked to me like he wanted me to stop."

Incredibly, instead of going into the standard home run trot, Allie screeched to a halt, pivoted, and slid back into second base in a cloud of dust. "I tore a hole out there getting stopped, and it was so big you could have buried a Mack truck in it," Reynolds said.

Not realizing he had whacked a home run, Allie hugged second base and ignored the pleas from the Yankee dugout to circle the bases. Even Senators second baseman Al Kozar urged him to finish his trot. "Since television started, all you guys want to be actors," he told Reynolds. Pointing to the bleachers, he added, "The ball is outta here."

Allie shook his head. "I'm not leaving," he said. "I've seen you guys talk people off bases before."

Neither Kozar nor shortstop Mark Christman could convince Reynolds to abandon his safe perch. Even when the umpire waved him on, Allie refused to budge. Finally, Yankees manager Bucky Harris convinced Allie that he had indeed hit a home run and that it was safe to leave second base.

"After they talked me off second, I finally got to do my home run trot, even if it was only halfway," Reynolds recalled. "Everyone in the place got a big laugh out of it—my teammates, the fans, even President Truman. He was laughing harder than anybody.

"I'll never forget that home run. First of all, it was the only one I ever hit in the big leagues. And second, after I hit it, I had to go and embarrass myself like that in front of the President of the United States."

The Five-Minute Double Play

Cesar Tovar of the Minnesota Twins was so bewildered and frustrated over his baserunning boner that he caused one of baseball's lengthiest double plays.

In a 1970 game against the Baltimore Orioles, Tovar took off from first on a hit-and-run as batter Rod Carew hit a fly ball to center. Tovar was past second when the ball was caught, but raced back to first in time to beat the throw. However, he failed to touch second on the way back, which the umpires failed to notice.

Baltimore manager Earl Weaver came out to protest. Meanwhile, Orioles first baseman Boog Powell told Tovar that he hadn't touched second. So Tovar ran over and slid into the base. Then, tired of all the embarrassment and hassle, he got up and went to the dugout.

Tovar's teammates yelled at him to go back to first, but Tovar said, "No way." The Orioles then threw to first and Tovar was out on a double play that took five minutes.

Clarence "Heinie" Mueller

**Outfielder • St. Louis-New York-Boston, N.L. • 1920–29
St. Louis, A.L. • 1935**

Emmett "Heinie" Mueller

Second Baseman • Philadelphia, N.L. • July 19, 1940

Although they weren't brothers, Clarence Mueller and Emmett Mueller had much in common. They shared the same name—Heinie Mueller—and the same reputation as baserunning bozos. They could have used coaches at every base, including home plate.

Clarence "Heinie" Mueller often boasted that, "I'm the only player who went from first to Houston on a pop foul."

It happened during a 1922 game when Mueller, playing for the St. Louis Cardinals, was perched on first base after stroking a single. The next batter popped up to the catcher a few feet behind the plate. But Heinie, with his head down, had been off and running with the pitch and wound up on third base when the ball was caught. Naturally, he was doubled off first. Cards manager Branch Rickey was so angry over the blunder that he put Mueller on a train to the Texas League farm club in Houston the next day for more seasoning.

In a game two years later, Mueller was leading off second base, totally oblivious to the fact that Cardinals teammate Chick Hafey was on third. Suddenly, Heinie took off in a misguided attempt to steal the already occupied base. When the dust settled and he realized his screw-up, Mueller told Hafey, "Chick, I got a hunch that one of us is gonna catch hell from Mr. Rickey . . . and I don't think it's you."

Mueller pulled some of his biggest baserunning boners *before* he ever reached first base. In a 1924 game against the Brooklyn Dodgers, Heinie whacked a screaming line drive off the shin of spitball pitcher Burleigh Grimes for an apparent base hit. But instead of running to first, Mueller charged toward the mound.

"You know what you can do with that damn spitter of yours!" Heinie yelled to Grimes.

The pitcher gave a wry smile, hobbled over to the ball, and threw to first for the out while Mueller was still standing in front of the mound, reading him the riot act.

Ed Brannick, New York Giants team secretary, recalled the time Mueller laid down a squeeze bunt. "Heinie bunted right in front of the plate. The catcher ran out and grabbed it and was all set for the runner coming down from third. However, that wasn't bad enough. . . . Heinie, instead of running to first, just stood there at home plate telling the runner to slide. So the catcher tagged out the guy trying to score, then turned around and tagged out Heinie, who was still standing there with his bat in his hand!"

When he retired from the game in 1935, it looked like baseball had seen the last of Heinie Mueller and his zany baserunning. But a few years later a new Heinie Mueller followed the zigzagging footsteps of the old Heinie.

In the fourth inning of a 1940 game against the St. Louis Cardinals, Emmett "Heinie" Mueller, of the visiting Philadelphia Phillies, drilled a base hit. The next batter, Johnny Rizzo, swatted a potential double-play ball to third baseman Jimmy Brown, who threw to second baseman Joe Orengo in an effort to force out Mueller.

Heinie, a five-foot, six-inch, 165-pound human bowling ball, rolled into Orengo as if the infielder were the lone ten pin. Orengo still winged the ball to first, hoping to nail Rizzo.

That's when all the fun started. Umpire Beans Reardon signaled that Mueller had beaten the throw to second. But there was one problem—Heinie didn't know he was safe.

Meanwhile, Orengo's relay flew over the head of first baseman Johnny Mize, so Rizzo scampered off toward second. Heinie, who had failed to see Reardon's safe signal, just assumed he was out and, with his head down, began trotting back toward the first base dugout. Suddenly, he noticed a streak of gray flannel passing him in the opposite direction.

Mueller stopped between first and second, trying to figure out what was happening. By now Mize had recovered the errant throw and had pegged the ball to Orengo, who slapped the tag on the befuddled Heinie.

Umpire Beans Reardon called him out and then turned to Rizzo, who was standing on second base, and called him out, too, for passing Mueller on the base path.

In the dugout Phils manager Doc Prothro moaned, "I just turned 47, but after plays like this I may not make it to 48."

Vince Coleman

Outfielder • St. Louis, N.L. • July 29, 1989

Vince Coleman once ran the bases as though he were a football player who was flagged for illegal use of the hands.

In the worst baserunning of his life, Coleman—the National League's No. 1 base stealer from 1985 to 1989—was called out twice for interference because he tried to win with his sneaky hands instead of his speedy feet.

In the third inning of a 1989 game against the Montreal Expos, Coleman beat out an infield single. Montreal pitcher Dennis Martinez then tried to pick him off first, but the throw was low. As Coleman dived back into first, the ball glanced off the glove of first baseman Andres Galarraga and hit the prone base runner on the leg.

As Galarraga reached down to pick up the ball, Coleman blatantly swatted it away into foul territory down the first base line and then sprinted toward second. A stunned Galarraga turned to umpire Eric Gregg and said, "Hey, I'm not chasing that ball."

Gregg immediately realized that Coleman had tried to pull a fast one and called him out for interference. "Vince, you can't do that," admonished the umpire. "Not even in the Pacific Coast League can you do that. What are you trying to do, win the game single-handed?"

Coleman didn't put up a fuss. He knew he had been caught red-handed. "I tried to get up and go and slap the ball all in one motion," he confessed later. "I made it too obvious. I guess I wouldn't make a good burglar."

Cardinals manager Whitey Herzog shook his head and said, "I've never seen a play like that in my life—in 40 years of professional ball." But he hadn't seen anything yet.

In the eighth inning Coleman again got on first with a hit. The next batter, Ozzie Smith, then rapped a double-play grounder to third baseman Tim Wallach, who fired the ball to second baseman Damaso Garcia. As Garcia made the pivot, Coleman brazenly grabbed hold of Garcia's shirt to stop him from relaying the ball to first.

Once again Coleman was called out for interference, this time by umpire John Kibler. Herzog dashed onto the field but put up little resistance. "Coleman said he didn't know he couldn't do that at second," said Herzog.

Admitted Coleman, "I swiped at him. I've seen runners take guys out at second by throwing their elbows." But ignorance of the law is no excuse. Coleman was guilty of two baserunning boners.

For a player who led the league in stolen bases for five years in a row, it was a frustrating week. The day before, he was caught stealing, ending a record-setting streak of 50 consecutive successful steal attempts. And three days before that, he was called out for cutting across the diamond trying to return to second base after he had gone too far around third on a fly ball.

After the game, which the Cardinals lost 2–0, Coleman said, "I cost us the game. I tried to do too much."

Living Up to His Name

The Brooklyn Dodgers were whipping the Pittsburgh Pirates 8–2 in the bottom of the eighth inning of a 1952 game when the Pirates' Rocky Nelson hit a triple.

On the next pitch Nelson broke for the plate in a barefaced attempt to steal home, and was thrown out by 20 feet.

When Nelson returned to the bench, Pittsburgh manager Billy Meyer asked him, "Why in the world would you try to steal home when we're down by so many runs?"

"Billy," said Nelson, shrugging his shoulders, "I guess that's why they call me Rocky."

Billy Rogell

Shortstop • Detroit, A.L. • 1934

To his everlasting embarrassment, Billy Rogell learned a good lesson: Never tick off an infielder because somehow, when you least expect it, he will get his revenge on the base path.

During the off-season, Rogell supplemented his modest Detroit Tigers salary by delivering milk in his hometown of Chicago for $41 a week. One of his customers was St. Louis Browns second baseman Oscar "Spinach" Melillo.

Because they were friendly rivals on the diamond, Rogell decided to have some fun at Melillo's expense during the winter. Rogell made sure that he delivered the milk to Melillo as early as possible, before six A.M. Rogell would put the milk on Melillo's back porch, rattle the bottles, and shout up to the bedroom window, "Here's your milk, Oscar!"

This never failed to wake up—and irritate—Melillo. Being a patient man, Melillo waited for his revenge. It came one day in 1934 when the Tigers were playing the Browns. With the score tied late in the game, Rogell slid into second with a double. Feeling happy about the hit, Rogell brushed the dirt off his uniform. Then he turned his attention toward the pitcher before taking a couple of steps off the base.

Melillo, playing second base, sauntered closer to the bag and said to Rogell, "Bill, remember how you'd wake me up in the morning by shouting, 'Here's your milk'?"

Rogell grinned and nodded. "Boy, do I. That sure made my day."

"Well, this is going to make my day," retorted Melillo as he tagged Rogell with the ball in the old hidden ball trick. "Now you've got some explaining to do to your manager. Who knows, you may wind up delivering milk again sooner than you think."

The following winter Rogell was somewhat quieter in his deliveries to the Melillo household. But he was determined to get the last laugh. In a recent interview, Rogell told how he got his revenge:

"Back then, the infielders used to leave their gloves on the field when they went in to bat. It just so happened I found a dead sparrow in the dugout, and I knew that Oscar was afraid of anything dead. So I put the dead sparrow on his glove. When he took his position in the field the next inning and saw that dead sparrow on his glove, he threw his glove in the air and took off running."

Daredevil Dave Altizer

Infielder • Chicago, A.L. • 1909

No base runner was ever duped more shamefully than Daredevil Dave Altizer.

Altizer, whose nickname reflected his bold running on the base paths, had just gone from the Cleveland Indians to the Chicago White Sox on waivers. Playing against his old club for the first time, Daredevil Dave was eager to make a good showing at Chicago's South End Park.

With the White Sox trailing 2–1 and one out in the bottom of the seventh inning, Altizer singled and immediately looked to third base coach Nick Altrock for the green light to steal. Altrock flashed him the hit-and-run sign.

On the next pitch, Daredevil Dave tore for second base. Unfortunately, the batter drove a sharp liner directly into the glove of first baseman George Stovall, who then stepped on the bag to complete the double play and retire the side.

But Altizer, whose back was to the play, had kept on running and was totally unaware that he had been doubled up. Meanwhile, Altrock—one of baseball's greatest funnymen—immediately recognized a golden opportunity for some laughs at Daredevil Dave's expense.

"Slide, Dave! Slide!" Altrock shouted. Altizer dutifully followed his coach's instructions as he slid into second. Then Stovall caught on to Altrock's little scam and deliberately threw the ball over the head of shortstop Terry Turner, who was covering second base.

"Third!" yelled Altrock. Scrambling to his feet, Daredevil Dave dashed for the base and again followed his coach's orders to slide. In the meantime, Indians center fielder Joe Birmingham recovered the errant throw and fired the ball to third baseman Bill Bradley, who obligingly let the ball get away from him and roll to the stands.

"Home!" shouted Altrock. A panting, dirt-covered Altizer climbed to his feet once again and raced for the plate. Bradley recovered the ball and threw it to catcher Nig Clarke, who had Daredevil Dave out by a mile. But Clarke purposely missed the tag as Altizer dove headfirst across the plate.

Umpire Billy Evans then climaxed the travesty by calling Daredevil Dave out at the plate. Altizer leaped to his feet and proceeded to manhandle the umpire in a way that would have banned the player for life if this had been anything but a practical joke.

He ranted and raved until a teammate dragged him away and told him the truth. As Daredevil Dave walked sheepishly toward the dugout, he turned to Evans and said, "I still insist I was safe at home, even if I was out at first."

Shameful Moments on the Base Paths

1988—Donnell Nixon of the San Francisco Giants tied a major league record when he was caught stealing twice in one inning. He was gunned down trying to swipe second base in the sixth inning against the Chicago Cubs. Later in the same frame, after the Giants batted around, Nixon was caught trying to steal home.

1985—Jeff Burroughs of the Toronto Blue Jays slid into second base and came to a dead stop six feet short of the bag and was tagged out. "Jeff just didn't have enough torque behind him," recalled teammate Jesse Barfield. "Shortly before the next game, we put down a base six feet in front of second just for Jeff."

1952—Trailing the Washington Senators 1–0 in the bottom of the ninth inning, the Boston Red Sox loaded the bases with one out and slugger Ted Williams at the plate. After the first pitch, Senators catcher Mickey Grasso picked off Walt Dropo at third base. On the second pitch, Grasso picked off Billy Goodman at first and ended the game.

1940—If ever a team did a magnificent job of putting itself out in an inning, it was the Brooklyn Dodgers in a game against the Boston Braves. In the first inning, Dixie Walker singled and was out trying to stretch it into a double. Babe Phelps singled and was out when he tried for third on Pete Reiser's single. Then Reiser was nailed when he tried to steal second base.

Bobby Murcer

Designated Hitter • New York, A.L. • May 29, 1982

The New York Yankees used Bobby Murcer as a designated hitter. What they really needed was a designated runner—for him.

Changing directions more times than a weather vane in a hurricane, Murcer ran his team into an embarrassing triple play.

In a game against the Minnesota Twins, the Yankees started the second inning off with singles by Murcer and Graig Nettles, two veterans who'd never be confused with any speed merchants. With Roy Smalley at bat and the count 3-and-2, Murcer broke for third and Nettles for second. Although the pitch was high and wide and would have been ball four, Smalley swung at it anyway and struck out.

Murcer, who hadn't stolen a base in nearly two years, was only about 20 feet away from third base when he screeched to a halt. He stunned everyone

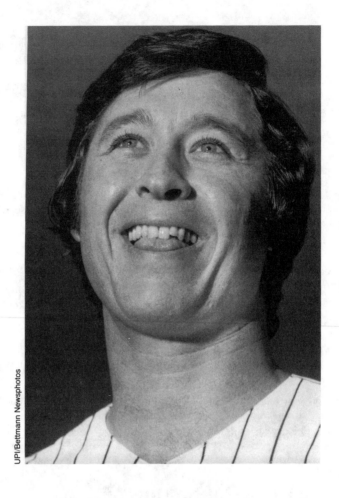

in the ball park when he suddenly wheeled around and retreated toward second. By this time Twins catcher Sal Butera had thrown the ball to third baseman Gary Gaetti, who began chasing Murcer. But Murcer managed to make it back safely to second base.

Except there was this one little problem. Nettles was already standing on second, having easily stolen what should have been his first base in four years. When Nettles saw Murcer arrive at second, Graig had no choice but to scamper back toward first. But Gaetti fired the ball to first baseman Kent Hrbek, who tagged Nettles for the second out.

Murcer couldn't leave well enough alone. Rather than stay safely perched on second, he decided he wanted to try for third base after all, and broke for that bag again. This time he went all the way. But long before Murcer arrived, Hrbek had thrown the ball to pitcher Terry Felton, who was now covering third. Murcer slid right into the tag for a weird 2–5–3–1 triple play.

New York coach Joe Altobelli couldn't believe his eyes. "Here we are trying to move people to keep out of a double play, and they get a triple play," he said, shaking his head.

When questioned by reporters after the game (which the Yankees won 6–4), Murcer gave a classic Hall of Shame explanation for his blundering baserunning: "Smalley struck out and caused havoc on the bases."

Showing how blame and shame were part of his game, Murcer said with a straight face, "I tried to deke them because I know Nettles isn't a gazelle on the bases. I was trying to keep me—the best runner of the two—from being out, so I could score from second."

Asked why he ran for third after forcing Nettles to run back to first, Murcer said, "Nettles was supposed to get in a rundown, but he messed up again. Now I've got to be here at seven in the morning to work on this play."

Coaker Triplett

Outfielder • Philadelphia, N.L. • July 11, 1943

Coaker Triplett wanted to show his new team how to play like a confident winner. Instead, he wound up looking like a bumbling loser.

He tried to steal an occupied base. That was bad enough. Even worse, he forced his teammate to run into an out. Coaker then stomped off the bag in disgust over his own blunder and was tagged out, too.

Triplett's baserunning fiasco occurred a few weeks after he had been traded by the speed-happy, world champion St. Louis Cardinals to the lackluster, cellar-dwelling Philadelphia Phillies. "The Cards were a cinch to win the pennant again, but I went to one of the worst teams in baseball," he recalled.

Coaker quickly discovered that his new teammates were so used to losing—they had finished in last place five years in a row—that they played with the vigor of tired old grandmas on a hot summer day. He figured the only way to inspire the Phillies on the base paths was to set an example for them. He wanted to show them how he ran the bases when he was with St. Louis. He set an example all right—a bad one.

In a game against the Cincinnati Reds, the Phillies were losing 6–0 when they mounted a feeble rally. With one out, Ron Northey walked. Triplett followed with another free pass, and Jimmy Wasdell dropped a single into right field to load the bases.

To Coaker this was the perfect opportunity to make something happen; to play the Cardinals way. Inching off second, Triplett set his sights on a stolen base. On the next pitch he broke for third. He slid in safely in a cloud of dust, only to find Northey standing on the bag with his mouth open in surprise. Coaker just assumed that Northey had scored on the previous play. Incredibly, Triplett never bothered to notice that third was still occupied.

"Get the hell off the bag!" screamed Coaker. Even though Northey had possession of the base, he obediently sprinted for home. But Reds catcher Moose Lakeman was waiting with the ball and easily tagged him out.

Shamefaced over his own blunder, Triplett stomped off the bag, kicking at the dirt and cursing his fate. Here he was, wearing the goat horns in front of his new teammates and a Shibe Park crowd that would boo a baby.

As Coaker continued to berate himself, Reds third baseman Steve Mesner— keeping a straight face—quietly summoned for the ball. When he got it, he walked over to the fuming Triplett and put the tag on him for a double play that ended the inning and quashed the rally.

Every Trick
in the Book

◆

To be a major leaguer, you first need to learn the basic fundamentals of the game, such as laying down a bunt, running the bases, and making the pivot on a double play. But to gain that extra edge that could mean the difference between winning and losing, players need to learn the finer points—how to doctor a baseball, dupe the umpire, or stretch the rules. For "The Sneakiest Chicanery Perpetrated by Players," The Baseball Hall of SHAME inducts the following:

Rennie Stennett

Second Baseman • Pittsburgh, N.L. • 1976

Pittsburgh Pirates second baseman Rennie Stennett pulled a sleight-of-hand trick that gave teammate Willie Stargell credit for a catch he never made.

In a 1976 game against the Los Angeles Dodgers at Three Rivers Stadium, Stennett hoodwinked everybody—including Willie—with his cunning chicanery.

A Dodger batter lifted a pop fly into shallow right field. Stennett and Stargell, who was playing first base, charged after the ball while right fielder Dave Parker raced in.

"I was probably in the best position to make the catch," recalled Stennett, "but I could feel the ground shaking with those two guys closing in. I wasn't going to get caught between them, so I pulled up."

While Stennett, who weighed only 160 pounds, moved out of the way, the 230-pound Parker and the 210-pound Stargell kept on coming. They both reached for the ball at the same time and crashed into each other in a collision that triggered tremors of Richter scale proportions. Unnoticed by everyone in the ball park, the ball dropped between them.

"They were pretty shaken up," Stennett said. "Dave was stretched out cold and Willie was groaning and trying to sit up. The ball was on the ground between them, but nobody else could see it. At first I was going to throw it in, but I knew I'd never get the runner in time. So I reached down like I was checking to see if they were okay and then I stuck the ball in Willie's glove.

"Willie was so dazed he didn't know what was going on. I told him, 'Come on, Willie, get up! Show them the ball!' "

Stennett's ruse worked like magic. As the umpire reached the crash site, Stargell staggered to his feet and held up his glove with the ball in it. The batter was called out and Stennett calmly strolled back to his position sporting the grin of the cat who ate the canary.

King Kelly

Outfielder-Catcher • Cincinnati-Chicago-Boston-New York, N.L. 1878–93

Hall of Famer King Kelly had the heart of a lion, the grace of a gazelle, and the conscience of a rattlesnake. When it came to ethics on the diamond, he struck out.

Although a player of immense talent, Kelly pioneered the idea that "anything is legal if you can get away with it." With a mixture of roguishness, cunning, and quick thinking, the King ventured into territory not covered by the rule book. In fact, his skill at discovering and exploiting loopholes kept league officials busy rewriting the rules.

Kelly was the first to pervert the rule that stated a player could be substituted at any time during the game by announcing it to the umpire. In an 1889 game against Cincinnati, Kelly, then captain of the Boston Braves, sat in the dugout while his backup, Charlie Ganzel, did the catching. Early in the contest a Cincy batter hit a high foul near the Boston dugout. Ganzel broke late for the ball and it was obvious he wouldn't be able to make the catch.

So Kelly leaped off the bench, rushed onto the field, and announced for all to hear: "Kelly now catching for Boston!" He then circled under the ball and caught it.

The play was legal, but officials soon closed that loophole. Now, of course, substitutions can only be made when the ball is dead and the umpire-in-chief has been notified.

Unlike other baseball blackguards, Kelly didn't stay awake nights plotting ways to skirt or break the rules. He was nimble-witted enough to hoodwink umpires and opponents on the spur of the moment.

In an 1887 game against the New York Giants, the King was patrolling right field for Boston as dusk descended in the ninth inning. New York, trailing by

a run, had the bases full and two out when Roger Connor laced a long, high drive to right in the dark. Kelly ran back to the fence, leaped, and made a grab for the ball. Then he triumphantly trotted off to the clubhouse as the umpire signaled the batter out. In the gathering gloom it seemed obvious to everyone that Kelly had made an amazing, game-saving catch.

In the clubhouse his teammates slapped him on the back and congratulated him. When a fellow Brave asked to see the ball, Kelly grinned and said, "It went way over the fence."

Back then, when the game was played with only one umpire, the King loved to bamboozle him. Whenever he was a runner on first and the batter hit to right field, Kelly would keep his eye on the lone arbiter. If the ump followed the progress of the ball, Kelly would cut across the diamond from first to third. The opposition would yell bloody murder, but to no avail, because the ump hadn't seen Kelly skirt second base.

When he was catching for Boston in an 1892 game against Cleveland, Kelly pulled off a little hoax to save the day. Late in a tie game with Cleveland's Jesse "The Crab" Burkett on second and two out, the batter swatted a base hit to left. In a fit of anger, Kelly dropped his mask and mitt at the plate as if the left fielder had conceded the run. Seeing this while rounding third, Burkett slowed to a trot. The left fielder then fired the ball to Kelly, who caught it with his bare hands and tagged out the startled Burkett.

"Never was there any other player in the game who had the brains to think of that play in the heat of action," marveled his contemporary, Hall of Famer Tommy McCarthy.

Kelly was always dreaming up trick plays, even while on the base paths. In a game against Detroit in 1886 when he was with the Chicago Cubs, the score was tied in the bottom of the ninth. With Kelly on second and teammate Ed Williamson on first, the pair executed a double steal.

Kelly then called time and, holding his arm, ran over to Williamson at second and announced loudly, "It's thrown out of joint, Ed. Take hold of it and pull on it."

But under his breath Kelly told him, "There's nothing wrong with it. Just listen to me. On the next pitch I'll start for home. I'll run slow so you can get around third and come in behind me. I want you to be right on my heels as I go to the plate. [Detroit catcher Charlie] Bennett will try to tag me, and just as he does, I'll spread my legs apart. You dive through my legs for the plate. He can't tag both of us at the same time—one of us is sure to score."

Just as he said, the play worked to perfection, giving Chicago the victory. King Kelly had just hornswoggled another opponent.

Russell Ford

Pitcher • New York, A.L. • 1909–1913

Russell Ford was the original mound doctor.

He invented the scuff ball and rode to fame with it before the pitch was banned by baseball.

In the spring of 1908 Ford was a minor league pitcher going nowhere. Then, by accident, he discovered the pitch that changed his life . . . and inspired future scuff ballers.

While warming up beneath the grandstands, Ford, a member of the Southern Association's Atlanta Crackers, threw a pitch that got away from catcher Ed Sweeney and struck a cement upright. After the ball was retrieved, Ford fired a fastball that jumped about a foot. When he got the ball back, Ford noticed that part of the ball had been roughed up from striking the grandstand.

It didn't occur to him that he had discovered one of the most baffling pitches a hurler can throw. Not until the following year did he try to throw the scuff ball in a game.

Between innings he used a broken pop bottle to roughen up the surface of the ball, and then walked out to the mound. "The dizzy contortions of that cut ball made me doubt my own eyes," he recalled years later. "I could see a distinct hop as the ball neared the batter, followed closely by a sideways sail. A double curve! Could any pitcher dream of a sweeter thing than that? Batters were missing my pitches by a foot."

Deciding to keep his discovery a secret, Ford looked for a way to scuff the ball without being detected. He settled on emery cloth and sewed a piece of it to the webbing of his glove. He also placed a disk of emery one inch in diameter on a ring he wore on his ungloved hand. That way, he could scuff the ball by rubbing it with either his hands or his glove.

Depending on how he gripped the ball, Ford could make the ball dip away or sail in on a batter. He won big in the minors and in 1910 made the roster of the New York Yankees.

When Ford was introduced to Yankee catchers Lou Criger and Jack Kleinow, he told them, "With me, you have to use two different fastball signs. One breaks down and away and the other sails in." The catchers laughed at the cocky rookie and wrote him off as a brash busher.

In his major league debut, the first three pitches Ford threw were scuff balls that the batter missed. Unfortunately, all three pitches eluded Kleinow as well, and the batter reached first. Yankee manager George Stallings was so livid that he yanked Kleinow. "Man, you must be drunk!" Stallings yelled at the baffled catcher. "You haven't put the glove on a single pitch yet."

When Criger went in to catch, he was a wide-eyed believer. Without hesitation he told Ford, "I'll give you two signs for the fastball. Anything you want."

Ford twirled a five-hit shutout and struck out nine as he beat the Philadelphia Athletics 1–0. He went on to win eight straight games with his emery ball—even beating the great Cy Young. Soon Ford was hailed as the game's newest pitching sensation. That year he hurled eight shutouts and finished with an incredible 26–6 record and an ERA of 1.65. The following season he posted a 22–11 mark with a 2.27 ERA.

But his stunning success didn't last. First, he suffered a sore arm and won only 25 games over the next two years. Then an inquisitive teammate figured out Ford's secret. When the player was traded to the Cleveland Indians, he told Indians hurler Cy Falkenberg how to throw the scuff ball.

Ford didn't know his secret had been revealed until he saw Falkenberg throw the scuff ball against the Yankees. Outraged by this betrayal, Ford actually stormed over to the Cleveland dugout between innings and accused Falkenberg of "stealing" his secret weapon.

"Who taught you how to throw my freak ball?" Ford asked.

"No one," lied Falkenberg. "That's a new one of my own."

"Well, you better do your best to keep it mum or there won't be any more batting averages because all the pitchers will start using it."

Falkenberg kept quiet and enjoyed his best season ever, posting a 23–10 record with a 2.22 ERA after winning only eight games the previous year. By now word had spread and pitchers everywhere were throwing scuffed-up baseballs.

But American League president Ban Johnson put a stop to the trickery by outlawing the pitch. It didn't matter much to Ford because his arm had gone bad and he had quit the game.

What he left behind was a legacy as the first pitcher to have the "right scuff."

How Dry I Am

The New York Yankees were convinced that Detroit Tigers pitcher Tommy Bridges often threw a spitball.

Before a 1941 game in which they faced Bridges, Yankees manager Joe McCarthy told his players to grab the ball if it ever popped out of the mitt of Tigers catcher Birdie Tebbetts. Then they were to present the ball to the umpire as evidence that Bridges was wetting it.

In the fourth inning, with Joe Gordon at bat, the pitch bounced away from Tebbetts. Gordon and the catcher dove for the ball and wrestled around near the plate. Tebbetts finally got possession and flung the ball to the outfield. By the time it was returned to plate umpire Bill McGowan, the ball had been handled by four Tigers and was as dry as the Sahara.

Shameful Moments in Chicanery

1957—During a game against the Milwaukee Braves the Cincinnati Reds had runners on first and second with no outs. Wally Post hit a double play ball to shortstop Johnny Logan. But Don Hoak, the runner on second, astonished everyone by fielding the ball. He knew he would be called out, because any runner who is hit by a batted ball in fair territory is automatically retired. But his clever ploy averted a double play. Hoak's trick led to a change in the rules. A similar play now would result in both the base runner and the batter being called out.

1933—Lew Fonseca of the Chicago White Sox laid down a bunt on the third base line. Knowing he didn't have a play, New York Yankees third baseman Joe Sewell used the spikes of his shoe to dig a 45-degree groove across the foul line. The ball rolled into the depression and went foul. A rule was immediately passed prohibiting such sneaky groundskeeping.

1920s—Bucky Harris, second baseman for the Washington Senators, used to lead the league in getting hit by pitched balls. He deliberately let himself get hit—and even wore leather padding strapped to his ribs to soften the blow of a pitched ball.

1902—Hatpin Harry O'Hagen, first baseman for the Chicago Cubs, got his nickname because of the extra piece of equipment he used on the field. He kept a large hatpin concealed in his glove. When a runner took a lead off first, O'Hagen would take the throw from the pitcher and tag the runner with the pin protruding from his glove. Even though the runner usually made it safely back to first, he would leap off the bag after being jabbed, and that's when Hatpin Harry tagged him out.

1890s—Pittsburgh Pirates catcher Connie Mack, who later became the Philadelphia Athletics longtime manager, was an expert at making a clucking sound that uncannily resembled a foul tip. On inside pitches or checked swings he uttered the cluck and tricked the umpire into calling the pitch a foul-tip strike.

Philadelphia Athletics

June 28, 1928

The Philadelphia Athletics pretended to act like choirboys while behaving like hooligans.

In a game against the New York Yankees in Philadelphia, the Athletics had the bases loaded with one out. Bing Miller of the A's then hit a high foul toward his club's dugout. Yankees catcher Johnny Grabowski tore after the ball and caught it a split second before he tumbled into the dugout.

Neither he nor the ball were seen for several seconds as Mickey Cochrane and Al Simmons, the runners on third and second, respectively, tagged up and scored.

Suddenly, Grabowski flew out of the dugout and ran up to umpire Tom Connolly. "Interference! Interference!" Grabowski shouted. Pointing to the A's dugout, he yelled, "Those bums ganged up on me. Call those runners back. I was interfered with after I made the catch."

Connolly, who saw nothing but a mass of humanity in the dugout after the catch, went over to the A's bench and appealed to their sense of fair play. "What about it? Did you interfere with Grabowski?"

"Hell no," said Jimmy Foxx. Flashing the look of an innocent schoolboy, he added, "Now we did grab him, but all we were doing was helping Johnny. Hell, if we hadn't reached out, he would've been in danger of cracking open his brains on the cement steps. We just caught him and cushioned him from a bad fall."

Grabowski couldn't believe what he was hearing. Facing the ump, he screamed, "It's a lie! It's a lie, I tell you. When I made the catch, one of those skunks tackled me around the ankles and I crashed into the dugout. When I went down, about six of these guys sat on me and I couldn't get up to make the throw."

"He's imagining things," said Foxx. "That's what we get for trying to help a fellow player. He's just mouthing off because he was out of position after the catch and forgot about the runners."

"Don't buy their story," screamed Grabowski. "They tackled me, sat on me, and kept me there until both those runners scored. Then they shoved me out."

Without evidence to the contrary, Connolly ruled that the runs counted. The A's managed to get away with the subterfuge and a 6–4 victory—and that sure didn't sit well with Johnny Grabowski.

Byron Browne

Center Fielder

George Altman

Left Fielder

Glenn Beckert

Second Baseman

Joe Proski

Trainer

Chicago, N.L. • March 28, 1966

The Chicago Cubs tried to steal a spring training game by resorting to some cloak-and-dagger trickery.

Then when they were accused of cheating, the sneaky Cubs perpetrated an underhanded coverup that even involved the team trainer.

In the second inning of a game against the San Francisco Giants at Phoenix, the Giants' Jim Ray Hart clubbed a deep drive that sent rookie center fielder Byron Browne racing back toward the wall. As he leaped, Browne crashed into the fence and the ball bounced about 20 feet away. It looked like a sure triple, or a possible inside-the-park home run.

Browne collapsed to the ground with the wind knocked out of him. But before he fell, he made an incredible play. Somehow, without moving more than a couple of feet, he quickly fired the ball to shortstop Don Kessinger, whose perfect relay throw to Ron Santo at third nipped Hart.

To the Giants it was unbelievable—too unbelievable. They had seen the ball bounce 20 feet away from Browne. Quickly solving the mystery, the San Francisco bullpen crew pointed to the prone Browne and shouted to the umpires, "He threw the wrong ball!"

Their cries brought Giants manager Herman Franks out of the dugout to protest. Meanwhile, Browne's concerned teammates rushed to his side—as much to join in a furtive fraud as to aid their fallen comrade.

They discovered that an extra ball, left over from batting practice, had remained unnoticed near the base of the wall when the game started. The injured Browne, unable to reach the game ball in time, had grabbed the worn practice ball instead and thrown it in.

So left fielder George Altman started a coverup. As he ran to Browne's side, Altman nonchalantly bent down, scooped up the game ball and stuffed it in his uniform. But this bit of chicanery did not go unnoticed. From the dugout Willie Mays, the Giants' eagle-eyed star, spotted Altman's subtle attempt at hiding the evidence, and Mays added his voice to the protesting chorus.

So Altman secretly slipped the ball into the glove of second baseman Glenn Beckert, who was kneeling by Browne's side. Beckert then surreptitiously handed the ball to trainer Joe Proski, who had rushed out to tend to Browne.

By now the entire Giants team was in an uproar, demanding the umpires take action against the Chicago con men. Finally, umpire Stan Landes waved his arms. "Everybody shut up!" he shouted. Turning to Cubs skipper Leo Durocher, the ump said, "Get all your guys over here and tell them to line up."

Landes then went down the line, frisking the Cubs one by one. Last in line was Proski, who had no one left to whom he could hand off the evidence. The red-faced trainer sheepishly forked over the game ball to Landes. The umpire compared it with the dirty, grass-stained ball that had been used to tag out Hart at third.

Landes then declared that the case of the switched balls had been solved. The umpire sent Hart back to second base with a ground rule double. And he sent the Cubs back to their positions in disgrace.

Jake Early

Catcher • Washington-St. Louis, A.L. • 1939–49

Jake Early was the motormouth of baseball.

Crouched behind the plate, the jabber-jawing catcher babbled, howled, hummed, and sang. He could yackety-yack the bat right out of the batter's hands, which was precisely why his tongue worked overtime. No catcher could distract a hitter better than Early.

Jake was the only backstop in the league ever to make Ted Williams laugh himself into an out. As one of the game's greatest hitters, Williams took pride in concentrating on each pitch. He usually could ignore all distractions.

But in one plate appearance the "Splendid Splinter" succumbed to Early's gift of gab. With each pitch, Jake imitated a country bumpkin, and was so funny that Williams dropped his bat in a fit of laughter and held his sides. Every time he stepped back into the batter's box, Williams began to laugh again, and took two strikes. On the 2–2 pitch, Jake launched into a rendition of "Turkey in the Straw." That did it. Williams cracked as the third strike sailed past him.

As noted sportswriter Shirley Povich wrote at the time, "Jake hath music to soothe the savage hitters."

The country singer was one of Early's favorite routines to disrupt the batter. He also loved doing imitations of a wild auctioneer and a play-by-play radio announcer.

The hot-air artist used the auctioneer bit to cool off the blistering bat of Washington Senators rookie Gil Coan. When he was brought up to the majors from Chattanooga at the end of the 1947 season, Coan had hit safely in every game and was batting .500. But then he fell victim to the chatter of Early, who was playing for the St. Louis Browns that year.

With his machine-gun delivery, Jake imitated a tobacco auctioneer, totally ruining Coan's concentration as the count went to 3-and-2. Then, as the pitcher wound up, Jake spouted the auctioneer's chant and kept it up until Coan swung and missed, whereupon Jake boomed from behind his mask, "Sold to Chattanooga!" By day's end Coan was wearing the collar.

When Early was on the Senators he often used the radio announcer routine to fluster Browns first baseman George McQuinn, who sported a .276 lifetime average. McQuinn would stand helplessly rattled at home plate as Jake whiffed him with words. "Here it comes, a high fastball," Jake intoned as the pitcher threw the ball, "and McQuinn takes it for a strike. . . . Now the windup, here's the pitch, and it's down the middle. McQuinn takes it with the bat on his shoulder for strike two. . . ."

By now McQuinn was in such a state of confusion, he was a strikeout waiting to happen. As the pitcher wound up, Jake screamed, "Here comes another fastball. McQuinn swings and misses." With a thud, a curveball sliced into Jake's mitt as McQuinn waved weakly at the pitch.

If ever a catcher deserved credit for striking out batters, it was Jake Early.

Tommy Murphy

Groundskeeper • Baltimore, N.L. • 1894

In one of the most blatant cases of chicanery ever pulled off by a nonplayer, Baltimore Orioles groundskeeper Tommy Murphy helped win a game for his team.

The Orioles, then in the National League, were hosting the New York Giants in an 1894 game at old Union Park. The score was tied 3–3 in the bottom of the ninth inning when the O's' Hughie Jennings came to bat.

Jennings banged a hot shot to Giants shortstop Shorty Fuller, who fumbled the ball and then, in an effort to whip it to first, threw wildly. The ball sailed over the head of first baseman Roger Connor, bounced off the front of the first base grandstand, and rolled with amazing speed toward the clubhouse entrance located just inside the short right-field fence.

Murphy was watching the game, sitting on the ground outside the clubhouse. As he cheered on Jennings, Murphy realized that the ball was heading straight for the clubhouse door. In a flash he opened the door, just seconds before the ball hit the steps, jumped up, and rolled inside. Immediately, Murphy followed the ball inside, slammed the door behind him, and locked it.

By this time both Connor and right fielder Silent Mike Tiernan arrived and found the door locked. Furiously, they tried to batter it down by hurling their bodies against it. They kicked at the door, hammered on it with their fists, and swore at Murphy.

Connor demanded that Murphy open the door, and threatened him with an unspeakable death if he didn't comply. But Murphy didn't budge. Not until he peeked out the clubhouse window and saw that Jennings had made it safely around the bases with the winning run did Murphy finally unlock the door. Then he poked out his nose, feigned surprise at seeing Connor and Tiernan there, and innocently asked, "Were you guys trying to get in?"

Connor, speechless at losing the game 4–3 because of Murphy's sneaky knavery, snarled, "You dirty, thieving crook! What do you mean by locking that door with the ball inside?"

"Oh, nothing, Roger," Murphy replied. "I was just playing a little inside baseball."

Philadelphia Phillies

June 9, 1906

The Philadelphia Phillies tried to win a game by resorting to the sneaky tactic of stalling. But their scheme was so blatant that they turned the game into a farce and a forfeit.

Playing at home against the Pittsburgh Pirates, the Phillies clung to a slim 1–0 lead going into the top of the eighth inning. As the Pirates came to bat, rain began falling from thick, low clouds that darkened the field.

Philadelphia manager Hugh Duffy urged umpire Bill Klem to call the game, claiming it was much too wet and dark to continue playing. But the ump refused and ordered the Phillies to take their positions. The Phillies knew that if they could stall until it was impossible to play, then Klem would be forced to call the game and the final score would revert back to the previous inning, giving Philadelphia the victory.

So the Phils turned the game into a shameful mockery.

Pittsburgh's Ginger Beaumont hit an easy grounder to shortstop Mickey Doolan, who deliberately muffed the ball. The next batter, Bob Ganley, laid down a sacrifice bunt that first baseman Ernie Courtney fielded cleanly and then dropped purposely so both runners were safe. The two Pirates moved up a base when pitcher Togie Pittinger uncorked a wild pitch. Both runners then scored on back-to-back singles by Fred Clarke and Honus Wagner as Pittsburgh took a 2–1 lead.

The rain began to fall harder as the Phillies continued their disgraceful stall. Pittinger hit Jim Nealon with a pitch, and then second baseman Kid Gleason deliberately fumbled Tommy Leach's ground ball. Claude "Little All Right" Ritchey then drilled a long drive, but center fielder Roy Thomas made no effort to go after the ball. Right fielder Silent John Titus picked up the ball and lobbed it to Doolan the shortstop, who promptly threw the ball high into the stands, clearing the bases. Pittsburgh widened its lead to 5–1.

Now it was the Pirates' turn to make the game even more of a farce. To defeat Philadelphia's stall, the Pirates tried to speed things up by getting themselves out.

Ed Phelps intentionally struck out. Vic Willis attempted to do likewise, but Pittinger drilled him in the ribs with a pitch. Pittinger then threw a wild pitch, but Willis remained on first base.

Umpire Klem had seen enough and ejected Pittinger. Duffy, the Philly skipper, then brought in infielder Joe Ward to pitch, but Klem wouldn't allow it. So Duffy summoned center fielder Roy Thomas to the mound, but the ump sent him back to the outfield. Klem threatened to eject Duffy if the manager didn't bring in a bona fide pitcher. So Duffy called for pitcher John McCloskey, who was in the clubhouse.

McCloskey took his sweet time sauntering to the mound. Once he got there, he hurled three straight warm-up tosses over the head of catcher Red Dooin, who slowly moseyed to the backstop to retrieve each one. Before McCloskey could throw a fourth bad warm-up pitch, he was given the heave-ho by Klem.

Hurler Johnny Lush then went to the mound and repeated McCloskey's tactics. That did it. Klem held up his hands and announced, "It's obvious that there's no way the side will be retired. This game is called."

But before the Phillies could celebrate, Klem shouted, "This game is not only over, it's forfeited to Pittsburgh!" The Phillies charged the ump and peppered him with vile epithets, but he ignored their rantings. Instead he strode off the field with this parting shot: "You tried to win by playing like losers. Well, you lost by playing like losers."

MOUND OF TROUBLE

◆

The pitcher's mound is where the hurler conducts his business.
Sometimes it's shady business and sometimes it's monkey business.
Other times the pitcher plays like he has no business being out there
at all. For "The Most Outrageous Performances by Pitchers," The
Baseball Hall of SHAME inducts the following:

Phil Marchildon

Pitcher • Philadelphia, A.L. • Aug. 1, 1948

Phil Marchildon threw the wildest wild pitch in baseball history. His errant pitch sailed into the tenth row of the grandstand and conked a fan smack on the noggin!

The Philadelphia Athletics' Canadian-born hurler was never known for his control. In fact, in his nine-year career he chalked up 203 more walks than strikeouts and twice led the American League in issuing the most free passes.

So it wasn't unusual for the right-handed Marchildon to uncork a wild pitch now and then. Even so, the one he flung in a 1948 game against the Detroit Tigers was a doozy that astonished even veteran players.

In the bottom of the fourth inning Detroit's Vic Wertz stepped up to the plate. Meanwhile, sitting in a tenth-row box seat between third and home, fan Sam Wexler of Toledo, Ohio, leaned over to light a cigar. Just then Marchildon went into his windup and cut loose with a pitch so wild that it flew into the grandstand and nailed Wexler right on the head.

Wexler didn't know what hit him. At first the Briggs Stadium crowd was hushed. But once they saw that the slightly dazed Wexler was not seriously hurt, they burst into raucous laughter.

"It was just a fastball that got away from me," Marchildon recalled. "I couldn't believe it went that far. It just sailed right into the stands and hit that poor fan."

Marchildon's teammates couldn't believe their eyes. "The first thing I thought was, 'Holy hell, what did I just see?' " recalled A's left fielder Barney McCosky. "I've never seen a wild pitch that wild before. I turned to [center fielder] Sam Chapman and he broke into a smile and shook his head."

Back on the mound the ears of the chagrined Marchildon were burning from the laughter. "Everybody was laughing—even my own teammates," he recalled. "I turned to [catcher] Buddy Rosar and said, 'I guess that was a little high.' Then I shouted to [plate umpire] Ed Rommel, 'You don't call 'em that high and outside, do you?' "

As for the beaning victim, Wexler was escorted by stadium ushers to the first aid room, but he didn't need any treatment. After thanking everyone for their concern, Wexler returned to his seat amid a big ovation from the crowd. Then he lighted a fresh cigar—while keeping a steady eye on Phil Marchildon.

A Ham on Wry

Cincinnati Reds relief pitcher Jack Billingham ordered one of baseball's most expensive sandwiches.

Even though there were strict team rules against eating in the bullpen during a game, Billingham offered a fan a couple of baseballs for a ham and cheese sandwich to be delivered to him in the bullpen in the fifth inning of a 1972 game in San Diego.

The fan agreed, but made the mistake of handing the sandwich to the batboy in the Reds dugout to give to Jack. Manager Sparky Anderson intercepted the sandwich and crushed it, wadded it up, and stomped on it. Then he told the batboy to give it to Billingham with the message: "The bill for this sandwich is 50 dollars."

Recalled Jack, "After Sparky got his grubby paws on it, I wouldn't have paid a nickel for it. The fine was bad enough. But I was starving out there and I didn't even get a crumb."

Dazzy Vance

Pitcher • Brooklyn-St. Louis-Cincinnati, N.L. • 1922–35

Hall of Fame hurler Dazzy Vance was often the victim of his own cockiness. He lost more games from a swollen head than from a hanging curve.

Usually Dazzy could back up his blatant bravado. The Brooklyn Dodgers' fireballing mound whiz led the league in strikeouts seven years in a row. But the colorful Dazzler admitted that sometimes his own loftiness sent him plunging to defeat.

Pitching for the Dodgers in a 1926 game against the Cincinnati Reds, Vance held a 1–0 lead in the seventh inning. The Reds had a runner on first and one out when five-foot, eight-inch second sacker Hughie Critz came to the plate.

"I always felt sorry for little Hughie," Dazzy recalled. "He was so small and helpless—leastways against me. On this day he hadn't hit the ball out of the infield in three tries. So I called catcher Hank DeBerry out to the mound.

" 'Hank,' I said. 'This poor little fellow is gonna bunt. He's so bad a hitter they'll make him bunt. But I'm a generous guy so I'm gonna feed him a real juicy pitch.'

"Critz hit it over the center-field wall for a home run. We lost 2–1."

By 1928 Vance was the highest paid pitcher in baseball, making all of $25,000. But his braggadocio once made him look like a two-bit batting practice pitcher when he faced the mighty New York Yankees in a spring training game.

In the hotel before the game, Vance introduced a country cousin of his to several of the Yankees. "This is Tony Lazzeri," said the Dazzler. "I'll strike him out. . . . This is Earle Combs. He'll pop up. . . . Meet Babe Ruth. He'll break his bat swinging at my stuff."

The Yankees didn't take too kindly to Dazzy's boastfulness. Leading off in the first inning, Combs did pop up just as Vance boldly predicted. But then Mark Koenig doubled, Lou Gehrig tripled, Ruth hit one out of sight, Bob Meusel tripled, and Lazzeri blasted another round-tripper, which sent the Dazzler to an early shower.

After the game, the cousin told Vance, "Boy, that's the easiest way to make $25,000 I ever saw."

Dazzy's arrogance extended to runners as well. He had a nifty pickoff move to first base and all but dared runners to steal on him.

Once, in a 1931 game against the St. Louis Cardinals, Vance was locked in a scoreless duel. In the bottom of the ninth the Cardinals had Pepper Martin on first and George Watkins on third with two out. Dazzy wanted to pick off Martin. Hoping to lull him, Vance threw softly to first base twice without showing his best pickoff move. After one more easy toss, thought Vance, he'd nail Martin with a great pickoff move. So Dazzy lobbed another throw to first—while Watkins, the forgotten runner on third, raced home with the winning run.

In 1934, when Vance was pitching for the Cardinals, he suffered what he called "the most disappointing game of my life." In the third inning against the Philadelphia Phillies, Dazzy belted a homer to put the Cards ahead 1–0. As the slim lead held up through the eighth inning, the cocky Dazzler was already putting another W in his personal win column.

"By the ninth inning I'm able to read the headlines in the next day's paper," he recalled. "I can see 'em as clear as if they'd already rolled off the presses: 'Vance's Homer Wins for Cards.' That headline screams in the biggest and boldest type since the sinking of the Lusitania.

"As I take to the mound in the ninth inning, I'm practically busting with pride. Except for Babe Ruth, no pitcher I ever heard of had won a 1–0 game with his own home run. Me 'n Ruth. The Dazzler and the Babe."

But in the bottom of the ninth the Phils put two runners on with a windblown pop-fly single and a scratch hit. "The headlines about Vance's homer winning the game aren't quite as sharp as they had been," recalled Dazzy. "I begin to revise downward the number of copies of the newspapers I had originally intended to buy."

The next two batters went down swinging. The headlines in Vance's mind sprang back to life. But then the next hitter skied a deep fly ball which got caught in a swirling wind. The ball dropped among three fielders as the tying and winning runs crossed the plate. "I lost the game 2–1, and those wonderful headlines never did get printed after all."

Double Trouble

Before a 1947 game against the New York Yankees, Washington Senators manager Ossie Bluege told pitcher Bobo Newsom to work carefully on slugger Joe DiMaggio.

"That guy must have a weakness, and I'm sure going to find out what it is," said Bobo confidently.

That afternoon DiMaggio lined three consecutive doubles off Newsom, the last of which sent the hurler to the showers.

After the game Bluege asked Bobo, "Well, did you find DiMaggio's weakness?"

"Yep," Newsom replied. "He's got a weakness for doubles."

Bobo Newsom

Pitcher • Brooklyn-Chicago-New York, N.L.;
St. Louis-Boston-Washington-Detroit-
Philadelphia-New York, A.L. • 1929–53

No pitcher ever suffered more injuries than Bobo Newsom. He was a walking calamity.

Throughout his 20-year career Bobo had more broken bones than a catacomb. Line drives bonked and conked him; wild throws bruised and contused him. Among his most important equipment were plaster casts and crutches.

Known as the Marco Polo of baseball, Newsom pitched on nine major league teams and changed uniforms 17 times. It didn't matter what the team colors were, his were always black and blue.

Adversity hounded him like a nasty bill collector. But Bobo was as tough as a battle-scarred drill sergeant.

His most talked-about injury occurred on Opening Day, 1936, when he was pitching for the Washington Senators against New York Yankees ace Lefty Gomez. The game meant a lot to Bobo because President Franklin Roosevelt, who had thrown out the first ball, was in the stands along with most of the Cabinet and the Supreme Court.

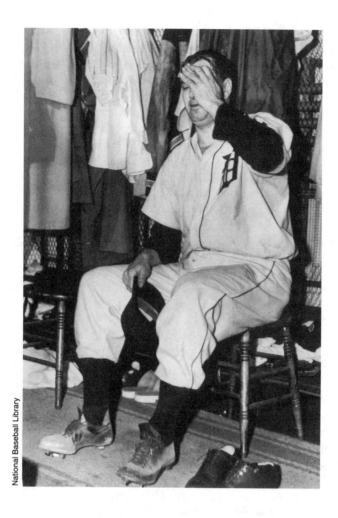

National Baseball Library

In the third inning Senators third baseman Ossie Bluege charged a slow roller, made a barehanded pickup, and fired a hard sidearm throw to first. The ball never got there. Watching from the mound, Newsom had become so enthralled with Bluege's fielding that he forgot to duck, and the ball struck him near his ear, breaking his jaw.

Bobo started running around in circles like a crazed, wounded animal before he toppled to the ground. Although he was out cold for a few seconds, Newsom made an incredible recovery and refused to leave the game. Despite the broken jaw, he went on to beat Gomez and the Yankees 1–0.

"When the President of the United States comes out to see ol' Bobo pitch, ol' Bobo ain't gonna let him down," said the hard-luck-but-tough-as-nails hurler.

The year before, Newsom was temporarily crippled by a wicked line drive off the bat of Cleveland Indians outfielder Earl Averill. "Just before it happened, we were kidding each other," recalled Bobo. "He said if I threw him an outside pitch, he'd hit it and knock me down. So I threw him an outside pitch, and he drilled one off my knee and cracked it up." Newsom went down like a tenpin, but he still managed to crawl to the ball and throw Averill out. Then the wounded hurler lay writhing and moaning.

Knowing that Bobo had a reputation as a clown, the Indians began laughing at him. That made him mad. Shaking himself loose from his teammates, who were about to assist him back to the clubhouse, Newsom limped back to the mound and finished the game (which he lost 5–4).

After the game, doctors discovered that his kneecap was shattered. He wore a cast for the next five weeks.

The broken kneecap and broken jaw were part of a long list of Newsom fractures that included legs, fingers, thumbs, and a collarbone.

Bobo had the lousiest luck both on and off the field. Driving to Chicago in 1932 to sign a contract with the Cubs, Newsom fell asleep at the wheel, drove his car off a Smoky Mountain road and dropped 225 feet. He was hauled out of the wreckage with a broken leg.

After a lengthy convalescence, Newsom, now free of his leg cast, was getting ready to join the Cubs. But before he left, he decided to visit a mule auction near his home in Hartsville, S.C. One of the mules, obviously not a Cubs fan, greeted the pitcher with a loud bray and a hearty kick—right to Bobo's recently healed limb, breaking it again.

In 1940, when he was with the Detroit Tigers, Newsom tripped in the dugout. He landed on the concrete floor and wrenched his back, putting him out of action for a few weeks.

Newsom wasn't always the victim of injuries. Sometimes he was the cause. In 1947 Washington teammate George Case was nursing an injured shoulder that was just about healed. One day, while Case was sitting on the bench, Bobo bounded into the dugout and absentmindedly gave Case a hard slap on the back. Case's shoulder was put out of commission again.

Hard Head

Cleveland Indians hurler Benn "Baldie" Karr let one of his fastballs get away from him, and it struck Boston Red Sox batter Ira Flagstead squarely over the eye in a 1926 game.

Flagstead just stood there rubbing the bruise as Karr rushed over to him and asked anxiously, "Are you hurt, Ira?"

"Nope, not at all," replied Flagstead.

Karr's concern suddenly changed to irritation. "Well, for the love of Pete," growled the pitcher. "Lie down, will you? It makes my fastball look pretty lousy when I hit a man squarely on the head and can't even hurt him!"

Lefty O'Doul

Pitcher • Boston, A.L. • July 7, 1923

Lefty O'Doul pitched his way into the record books—the shameful way. In what has been called the "Indian massacre," Lefty surrendered more runs in one inning than any pitcher in major league history.

Before he could retire the side, O'Doul was clobbered for an incredible 13 runs! What made it even more painful was that all the runs came after two were out.

On a hot July afternoon the visiting Boston Red Sox took on the Cleveland Indians. Lefty, who had been used sparingly by Boston as a middle reliever and mop-up man, sat in the shade of the bullpen, hoping to see some action.

He soon got more than he ever bargained for. With the Sox trailing 8–0 at the end of three innings, manager Frank Chance summoned O'Doul to the mound. Chance figured the young hurler couldn't do any worse than starter Curt Fullerton. Chance was dead wrong.

Lefty gave up a run in the fourth and two in the fifth. Then came his Armageddon. While getting two outs, he filled the bases with two walks and a single. The inning would have ended quietly if O'Doul hadn't been victimized by bad luck. Boston center fielder Leaping Mike Menosky muffed Luke Sewell's fly ball, allowing two runs to score.

When those things happen, good pitchers simply concentrate on the next batter. But not Lefty. Fuming over his teammate's error, O'Doul threw fat pitches to Riggs Stephenson, who doubled in a run, and to Rube Lutzke, who singled in two more. Lefty was becoming unraveled. He walked Frank "Turkeyfoot" Brower and also Steve O'Neill. The bases were now loaded for opposing pitcher Stan Coveleski, an .089 hitter. Surely, O'Doul thought, he could escape further embarrassment by getting Coveleski out. But the way Lefty was pitching, Coveleski looked like Ty Cobb at the plate and smashed a two-run single.

Having been raked for seven runs in the inning, Lefty gazed over to the dugout, waiting and hoping Frank Chance would yank him. But with the score 18–2 at this point, the Sox skipper knew the game was lost. All that remained of interest was how many more runs O'Doul would surrender in the wild inning.

Like a lone soldier caught in an ambush, Lefty continued to get bombed. He walked Charlie Jamieson to load the bases again for Coaster Joe Connolly, who drilled a two-run single. After walking Ray Knode to refill the bases,

O'Doul yielded another two-run single to Sewell. Then Stephenson rocked Lefty for a booming double that drove in the 12th and 13th runs of the inning. The assault finally ceased, through no help of O'Doul. As the *Cleveland Plain Dealer* reported, "With his teammates all fatigued from a half hour of running, [Stephenson] tried to steal third and was flagged for the third out."

The shell-shocked O'Doul staggered off the mound, having etched his name in the record books by giving up 13 runs, seven hits, and six walks in one frame—a dubious feat which the newspaper declared would "be epochal for many a day."

Said the *Plain Dealer:* "The Tribe staged an almost endless procession over the groaning and cruelly dented plate. The Indians attack was so vicious and so unending that Frank Chance [changed] pitchers only when [O'Doul] became too tired to throw any longer." The Indians went on to massacre the Red Sox 27–3.

O'Doul had seen enough of the pitcher's mound. When the season ended, he vowed never to pitch again. Inspired by the glee on the Indians' faces during their hitting spree against him, Lefty figured it was more fun to bat than to pitch.

He went to the minors, learned to be a hitter, and returned to the bigs five years later. The following season, 1929, Lefty led the league in batting with a whopping .398 average. He battered opposing pitchers the way he was battered on that fateful day in Cleveland.

Shameful Mound Conversations

1969—Seattle Pilots manager Joe Schultz went out to the mound to give the hook to pitcher Fred Talbot, who was getting shelled. Talbot complained, "Where in the world have you been? I thought you'd never get out here."

1965—When New York Mets manager Casey Stengel visited the mound to lift Tug McGraw, the hurler begged, "Let me pitch to one more man. I struck him out the last time I faced him." Stengel shook his head and said, "Yeah, but the last time you faced him was in this same inning."

1959—With the bases loaded in a game against the Detroit Tigers, New York Yankees rookie pitcher Mark Freeman went into his windup, stopped, and staggered around the mound holding his eye. The umpires called a balk. When manager Casey Stengel asked him what happened, Freeman explained, "I couldn't help it, Casey. A bug flew in my eye." Stengel retorted, "Dammit. If you're gonna pitch in the majors, you are gonna have to learn to catch 'em in your mouth."

1934—In the first game of the World Series, St. Louis Cardinals pitcher Dizzy Dean summoned player-manager Frankie Frisch to the mound before facing Detroit Tigers slugger Hank Greenberg. "What was that pitch you said not to throw Hank?" Dizzy asked. Replied Frisch, "His power is high inside fastballs." A moment later Greenberg blasted a homer into the center-field seats. Dean turned to Frisch and said, "Frank, you were right. That's where his power is, all right."

Dizzy Dean

Pitcher • St. Louis, N.L. • May 19, 1937

Dizzy Dean committed the most notorious balk in baseball history. Because of the infraction, Dizzy lost his temper, the game, and a wild protest.

Shortly before the game, umpire George Barr talked with the starting pitchers, Dean of the St. Louis Cardinals and arch rival Carl Hubbell of the New York Giants. Barr warned them that the league office had ordered umpires to diligently enforce the balk rule. He reminded the hurlers that when they go into their stretch they must come to a complete stop.

Dean nodded nonchalantly and didn't give the balk talk another thought until it was too late. In the early innings he committed two balks, but Barr didn't call them. Instead, the ump told Cardinals catcher Mickey Owen to warn Dizzy that the next balk would be called.

Dean paid little heed. He was pitching masterfully and holding on to a 1–0 lead in the sixth inning when New York's Burgess Whitehead singled and was sacrificed to second base. The next batter, Dick Bartell, lifted a pop fly to shortstop Leo Durocher. But the play didn't count because Barr ruled that Dizzy had balked on the pitch for failing to "pause momentarily" during his stretch. Whitehead was waved to third base and Bartell was returned to the batter's box.

An outraged Dean threw down his glove and charged the ump. He and his teammates swarmed around Barr, kicked dust on him, and chewed him out. But the arbiter stuck to his guns. Dizzy was so furious he stormed into the dugout and threatened to quit on the spot. He was finally persuaded to play, but not before he harangued the ump some more.

Dean never found his lost composure. The fuming-mad hurler flung fastballs right down the middle, and the Giants responded with four hits and three runs in the inning.

As the game wore on, Dizzy's smoldering rage rode on every pitch as he brushed back the batters. Every Giant hit the dirt. In the ninth New York batter Jimmy Ripple barely escaped a beaning. To get even, Ripple bunted down the first base line, and when Dizzy covered the bag, the two collided.

In a split second Dean and Ripple were swinging fists and both dugouts emptied in a tempestuous 15-minute battle. "Players were swarming on the field like flies," said the Associated Press. "A half-dozen private fights started, the men rapping out good clean singles off each other's anatomies. The police, the umpires, and other outside help finally restored order."

Incredibly, Dizzy—the real cause of the free-for-all—not only walked away without a scratch, but was permitted to continue pitching. Ripple returned to first base because he had never been tagged out on the play that ignited the melee.

Dean proceeded to nail Jack McCarthy, the first batter since the fight, with a fastball. Then the hotheaded hurler gave up a run-scoring double and lost the game 4–1.

But that wasn't the end of Dizzy's fury over the balk call. Dean, whom league president Ford Frick fined $50 for fighting, was still simmering four days later when he took the mound against the Philadelphia Phillies.

In the second inning Dizzy tried to make a travesty of the "momentary pause" ruling. With a runner on first, he went into his stretch—and stayed frozen in that position for *three minutes* before pitching to Jimmy Wilson.

When Dizzy took an intolerably long four minutes to throw from the stretch on the next pitch, plate umpire Beans Reardon threatened to call a balk. The arbiter claimed that a balk can be called on a pitcher who holds a ball so long as to delay the game unnecessarily.

"All right," sneered Dizzy. "What do you want me to do? Pitch right through the stretch as I did the other day? Or wait, as I'm doing now? Make up your mind." Then Dean plopped defiantly on the ground and staged a sit-down strike while the umpires and Cardinals manager Frankie Frisch argued over the balk rules. After the brouhaha ended, Dizzy cooled down and pitched a 6–2 complete-game victory.

None of Dean's balky turmoil would have occurred if it hadn't been for his own manager. Ironically, just a week earlier, Frisch joined other National League pilots in demanding to Frick that the balk rule be rigidly enforced!

What Goes Around Comes Around

In a 1946 game, Detroit Tigers ace Dizzy Trout struck out Boston Red Sox slugger Ted Williams with the bases loaded in the bottom of the ninth to win 4–3.

Dizzy was understandably overjoyed. His catcher, Bob Swift, shook his hand and gave him the ball. After a quick shower, Trout went to the Boston clubhouse and asked Williams to autograph the ball. Williams obliged.

Two weeks later Williams blasted a tremendous three-run homer off Trout. As he rounded first base Williams hollered to Dizzy, "If you can get the ball back, I'll sign that one for you, too."

UMP CHUMPS

◆

Umpires are necessary evils, like batting slumps, bad-hop singles, and cold hot dogs. Without them, what would fans have to complain about? Grudgingly, we must admit that umpires are pretty honest fellows. It's just that the men in blue occasionally screw up and strike out like the rest of us. For "The Craziest Actions of Umpires," The Baseball Hall of SHAME inducts the following:

Ron Luciano

American League • June 1, 1971

Ron Luciano looked more like Hulk Hogan than an umpire when he flattened New York Yankee shortstop Gene Michael and put him out of action for several days.

Luciano, one of the most flamboyant arbiters to ever don the blue, was umpiring at second base in a 1971 game between the Yankees and the Oakland Athletics at Yankee Stadium. In the top of the ninth inning the A's' Joe Rudi singled and got the sign to steal.

On the pitch, Rudi took off for second, Michael ran over to cover the base, and Luciano rambled into position to make the call. However, catcher Thurman Munson's peg was wide toward the first base side of the bag.

Michael, Rudi, the ball, and 220 pounds of charging umpire arrived at second at about the same time. Michael caught the throw as Rudi slid in safely beneath him.

In his own inimitable style, Luciano gave a Broadway performance as he theatrically spread his hands in the safe sign. But one man was out—Gene Michael.

The shortstop sailed through the air just as the ump was giving the safe sign. Luciano's battering-ram forearm and elbow slammed into Michael's head and laid him out flat. "One minute Gene flashed by me, and the next

minute he was out for the count," recalled Luciano. "I mean, I nailed him but good."

The lights went out for Michael for several minutes. When he was revived, he was too woozy to stand and had to be carried off the field on a stretcher. Michael was rushed by ambulance to the hospital, where he was treated for mouth lacerations and a severe case of whiplash. He was fitted with a neck brace and ordered to sit out for a few days.

"I didn't know what happened," Michael recalled. "I got hit, then my head started hurting. I couldn't figure it out."

When he returned to the Yankees lineup, he saw that Luciano was once again the second base umpire. So Michael took up his position at deep short—as far away from Ron "The Hit Man" Luciano as he could get.

Bill Guthrie

National League • 1913; American League • 1928–32

Bill Guthrie was the "dis and dat, dem and dose" umpire.

He had a tongue that silenced protesting players and managers with a unique blend of humor and other-side-of-the-tracks English.

For example, in a 1932 spring training game, Cincinnati Reds first baseman Mickey Heath fanned on three pitches. On his next at-bat he swung and missed at the first two pitches. Guthrie called the next pitch strike three.

"You missed that last one, Bill," said Heath.

"Well, Mickey," retorted Guthrie, "if youse can miss five of dem, I oughta have de right to miss one."

Bill umpired for 40 years, mostly in the minors. Although his stint in the majors was relatively brief—only six years—no one who ever saw him could ever forget him. With a mammoth torso, slender bowlegs, and an imperious strut, Guthrie always made his presence felt. Few questioned his judgment.

65

When they did, he usually turned their protests aside with a quip that left them speechless.

Guthrie had a sure-fire formula for avoiding arguments with irate managers, coaches, and players.

"Nuttin' to it," the colorful ump explained in his butchered English. "I calls the guy out. He jumps up and yells, 'Whaddaya mean, out?' And I says right back to him, 'Das what I mean, out!' And den I walks away from him wid me arms bowlegged, like dis." Whereupon Bill went into the famous Guthrie strut, a tough swagger where his bowed arms and legs made him look like a fearsome figure eight.

Guthrie would let a player make his complaint—known in those days as a "kick"—but the umpire wouldn't tolerate any histrionics. As Bill used to say, "Dose short kicks I don't mind. But when dey give me dem banquet speeches, dey're t'rough!"

Once, in 1930, the Boston Red Sox were riding Guthrie unmercifully from the dugout. He finally got so incensed that he cleared the bench of all players. As he returned to his position behind home plate, Guthrie turned to third base coach Heinie Wagner and snapped, "And youse is out of de game, too!"

"Me?" protested Wagner. "I didn't say anything."

"No, but youse was t'inking."

"How do you know I was thinking?"

"Well, I give youse credit for it anyway. Now git out!"

Then there was the time in 1932 when veteran Philadelphia Athletics third baseman Jimmy Dykes protested to Bill over a called strike. "Pipe down, kid," said the gruff but witty ump, "and nobody but youse and me and de catcher will know youse can't see anymore."

Another time, Guthrie called a strike on A's outfielder Doc Cramer, who squawked, "That was a bad ball, Bill."

"Bad ball?" asked Guthrie. "Say, kid, I just took it out of de ball bag."

Cramer singled on the next pitch and moved to third on another hit. He tried to score on an infield roller but was called out at the plate. Again Cramer protested, this time saying the catcher missed the tag.

"Say, what do youse want a catcher to do—knock you goofy when he tags youse?" asked Guthrie. "Youse is out. Furdermore, no back talk."

George Hildebrand

American League • Aug. 1, 1928

In one of the most embarrassing moments ever experienced by an umpire, George Hildebrand was forced to ask a player to call himself out—because the ump didn't see the play.

It happened during the first inning of a game between the visiting New York Yankees and the St. Louis Browns. Back then, only two umpires worked the bases. After disposing of the first two Yankees, Browns pitcher General Al Crowder gave up a homer to Babe Ruth and a walk to Lou Gehrig. As New York's Bob Meusel stepped to the plate, Hildebrand moved to a position between first and second.

Meusel hit a grounder to shortstop Red Kress, who scooped the ball up swiftly and gracefully and prepared for an underhand toss to second baseman Otis Brannon. It was an easy and obvious play—so obvious that Hildebrand kneeled on one leg to get a good view of second to make the call.

Seconds passed, yet nothing happened at second base, other than that Gehrig was now standing on it. Hildebrand felt a sickening sensation in his stomach. He turned around to see Meusel on first base and Browns first sacker Lu Blue with the ball. Kress had changed his mind and thrown to first because Brannon was late getting over to second for the force play.

The teams and the fans in the stands had seen Meusel get thrown out by 30 feet at first. But Hildebrand flat-out missed it. And it's always been a cardinal rule that an umpire can't call what he hasn't seen.

The chagrined arbiter turned to his partner, Bill Guthrie, behind the plate, and asked him to make the call. But Guthrie confessed that at the time of the play, which looked so obvious to everyone, he was stooping over to clean the plate.

The St. Louis crowd began to yammer because, after all, Meusel had been retired and the inning should have been over. Yet there was Meusel still glued to first. The Browns, led by their manager Dapper Dan Howley, rushed up to Hildebrand and demanded that he call Meusel out. Meanwhile, in the dugout, the Yankees were holding their sides with laughter.

Out of desperation, Hildebrand swallowed his pride, walked up to Meusel, and said, "Everybody knows you're out, Bob. Everybody saw it. . . ."

"Everybody but the umpires," replied Meusel with a pleasant sneer.

"So be a sport," the respected veteran umpire pleaded, "and call yourself out."

Meusel managed a wry smile. "George, you've been getting nine thousand bucks a year for a long time as an umpire. Now's a good time to start earning it."

Hildebrand had no choice but to order the Browns to return to their positions and resume play. Crowder trudged back to the mound, whereupon he got New York's Tony Lazzeri to pop up for the *fourth* out of the inning.

Jim McKean

American League • Aug. 4, 1985

Umpire Jim McKean helped the Detroit Tigers turn a key hit into an inning-ending double play.

In the seventh inning of a game against Detroit, the visiting Milwaukee

AP/Wide World Photos

Brewers had runners Jim Gantner on second base and Charlie Moore on first with one out. Paul Molitor then hit a sinking liner to left fielder Larry Herndon, who raced in for an attempt at a shoestring catch. Gantner, thinking that Herndon had caught the ball, retreated to second base. He arrived just in time to find Moore standing there.

Herndon then fired the ball to shortstop Lou Whitaker, who, seeing two Brewers on the bag, tagged Gantner. But McKean, who was umpiring at second, pointed to Gantner and shouted, "You're safe!"

Convinced that McKean had ruled Herndon had definitely caught the ball, Moore did the only thing he could. He took off in fast retreat toward first and made it safely, only to discover that Molitor was already there. Moore didn't know where he belonged until he learned that Herndon had actually trapped the ball. But by then it was too late and Moore was called out.

After a long debate with Brewers manager George Bamberger and a conference with the other umpires, McKean realized he had blundered. Since the ball had never been caught, the ump knew that Moore, not Gantner, had rightful possession of second base. So McKean ruled that Gantner now was out.

"Why did you call me safe?" said Gantner.

McKean confessed, "I called you safe before I found out the ball wasn't caught. I assumed it was caught because Herndon threw to second."

Then Moore charged McKean and demanded to know why he was called out. "Even though I motioned Gantner safe," explained the chagrined umpire, "you were still on your own." Since Molitor had possession of first base because of his single, Moore had been ruled out.

"Let me get this straight," said Moore. "You've admitted you were wrong. Yet you're going to punish us for your two mistakes?" McKean nodded sheepishly.

"If you called Gantner out like you were supposed to do, then Charlie would have stayed on second," Bamberger told the ump. "You forced our man off the bag."

Instead of having the bases loaded with one out, or at least runners at first and second with two out, the Brewers were out of the inning.

"I'm playing this game under protest," announced Bamberger.

Tigers manager Sparky Anderson, an expert on the rule book, then joined the rhubarb and told the umpires, "Don't worry about that protest. Bamberger's protest won't stick. But if you don't call both of them out, you'll have a protest by me that will hold up.

"But don't include me in your troubles. If he [Moore] is dumb enough to believe you, that's his problem."

Bamberger claimed the bizarre play cost the Brewers a victory in what ended up as a 7–4 loss to the Tigers.

A few days later, American League president Bobby Brown ruled against Bamberger's protest.

With tongue in cheek, a smirking Sparky Anderson gave the Brewers this piece of advice: "You just can't put your trust in umpires."

James Lincoln

National League • 1913

Umpire James Lincoln was the target of such verbal abuse from players that he quit his job—after only one game!

In 1913 National League president Thomas Lynch hired Lincoln, an instructor at Harvard, to umpire during the summer. Lynch had watched Lincoln umpire college baseball games and was impressed with his scholarly bearing. Lynch thought that Lincoln could give big league umpiring a needed touch of dignity.

In his major league debut, Lincoln was teamed up with veteran umpire Bill Klem for a game between the Boston Braves and the visiting New York Giants. Before the game Klem gave the rookie umpire some last-minute pointers.

"Don't worry about me, Mr. Klem," said Lincoln in a voice brimming with confidence. "I'll make the players respect me and I'll keep the situation well in hand at all times."

Things went along smoothly until the third inning, when the Giants launched a rally that was squelched after Lincoln made a call on a bang-bang play that went against New York. Suddenly, Giants manager John McGraw and his players began to work on Lincoln. They questioned his eyesight, they complained about his judgment, they assailed his ancestry.

With each inning the verbal assault on the new arbiter intensified. Lincoln, his face growing a darker shade of red with each stinging remark, finally could take no more guff. He halted the game, strode over to the Giants dugout, and declared, "I shall not tolerate such vile language. Either you act like gentlemen or leave the park."

McGraw just scoffed at him and then snarled, "Go back to the classroom and teach the kids their ABC's. Leave the umpiring to guys who know their business." His players broke into derisive laughter.

The irked Lincoln spun on his heels and returned to his position. His attempt to silence the Giants merely spurred them to barrage him with even more bench jockeying. They blasted Lincoln with every foul name they had ever heard. But the stoic ump endured the tongue-lashing to the bitter end.

When the game, which New York lost, was over, the Giants surrounded Lincoln. They cursed him. They shoved him. They stepped on his feet with their spiked shoes.

Klem finally rescued Lincoln and hustled him off to the dressing room. "Well," said Klem, "how did you like your first day of umpiring professional baseball?"

"It's a horrible business, Mr. Klem," replied Lincoln. "I don't want to talk about it."

After changing his clothes, Lincoln opened the door to the dressing room and heard Klem shout, "I'll see you tomorrow."

But Lincoln never responded. That was the last time Klem or the rest of the National League ever saw of him.

Bill McGowan

American League • 1925–54

Bill McGowan intimidated rookies, silenced veterans, and vexed everyone.

McGowan once fined and ejected a player and manager for protesting a call that he admitted to them he had blown!

Working a Cleveland Indians game in 1938, McGowan called a ball on a pitch that cut through the heart of the strike zone. Indians pitcher Johnny Allen leaped off the mound and shouted to Bill, "That ball was right over the plate!"

"Sure, it was right over," the ump admitted arrogantly. "So what? I called it a ball, so it's a ball."

Allen exploded in such a rage that McGowan threw him out of the game and fined him $25. Then manager Oscar Vitt charged out of the dugout to protest.

"You can't throw Allen out for putting up a beef because you missed the pitch," claimed Vitt. One word led to another, and Vitt was given the thumb and a $25 fine, too.

Later, in the clubhouse, Vitt told reporters, "That's one for the book, isn't it? A pitcher cuts the plate with a strike, the umpire calls it a ball, then admits it was right down the middle, and then fines the pitcher and manager for daring to open their mouths. What is this, anyway, Russia?"

The first player McGowan ever threw out was Babe Ruth, and the ump did it in a misguided effort to demand respect. It happened at Yankee Stadium in 1925 when Bill was a rookie umpire and Ruth was baseball's superstar. The Babe protested a called third strike—but without the rancor normally required to get ejected—yet McGowan gave him the old heave-ho.

The Babe, blinking in disbelief that a rookie arbiter would dare to toss him out of the game for so minor a transgression, asked, "Do you know who I am?"

"I know who you are and all about your reputation," Bill snapped. "But when I'm wearing this blue suit, you're just another ball player to me. Now get out."

McGowan literally terrorized rookies into respecting him. In a classic case of intimidation, he showed how to bully a young player out of ever uttering the simplest protest. In a 1953 game the Boston Red Sox's rookie outfielder Tommy Umphlett was called out on strikes. McGowan didn't just say "strike three." Instead, he stepped from his position behind the catcher, stuck his chin under Umphlett's face, waved a doubled fist under the batter's nose, and then thundered, "Strike three!"

McGowan got the desired respect for authority when Umphlett replied meekly, "Yes, sir," and walked quietly back to the dugout.

Bill wasn't afraid to inject humor into a budding argument. In 1938 Jimmy Dykes, then player-manager of the Chicago White Sox, was leading off second with the bases loaded and one out in a game against the Detroit Tigers. Suddenly, Tigers catcher Rudy York fired the ball to Charlie Gehringer at second. Dykes was picked off cleanly.

"Out!" shouted McGowan.

"No, no," said Dykes. "I made it. I got back."

"Yes, you did, James," McGowan replied politely. "You made it back . . . but what detained you?"

Another time, Bill was working behind the plate in Yankee Stadium when he called Yogi Berra out on strikes. Manager Casey Stengel bolted out of the dugout to challenge McGowan, but then thought better of it and turned to Yogi and asked, "Was that a good strike?"

"Well, I don't know, Casey," Berra replied. "I really didn't get a good look at it."

Then McGowan stepped in and said, "Gentlemen, I had a full view of the pitch. It was a thing of beauty. It took about two inches off the outside corner, and I will further say that it was a very fast ball. That is my considered opinion, gentlemen, and I will not change it."

McGowan took his umpiring so seriously that when he entered the American League in 1925 he did homework in his hotel room. For hours on end he stood in front of a mirror and shouted, "You're out!" He did it again and again, only with different inflections and gestures.

One night a booming voice came through the wall from the next room, shouting, "Hey, don't you ever call anyone safe?"

That's the Way the Rookie Crumbles

◆

Aspiring major leaguers dream about what their first year in the bigs will be like. They see themselves as phenoms who hit game-winning homers and make game-saving catches. That's the fantasy. The reality is that in their first days in the bigs, rookies often stumble over their feet, fall flat on their faces, or otherwise embarrass themselves at the beginning of a career that can be a whole lot shorter then they'd ever planned. For "The Most Inauspicious Major League Debuts," The Baseball Hall of SHAME inducts the following:

Mickey Mantle

Center Fielder • New York, A.L. • March 11, 1951

Everybody raved about Mickey Mantle, the new kid on the block with blazing speed and a thundering bat. But the raves turned to raspberries when the much-ballyhooed rookie zeroed in on the first fly ball hit to him as a major leaguer—and got smacked right between the eyes.

Mantle arrived at the New York Yankees temporary spring training base in Phoenix in 1951 as the heir-apparent to Hall of Famer Joe DiMaggio. Brought up as a shortstop, Mickey was immediately shifted to the outfield by manager Casey Stengel, who was impressed with Mickey's speed and powerful arm.

Former Yankee outfielder Tommy Henrich was assigned the job of teaching Mantle the tricks and treacheries of the outfield. Henrich had his work cut out for him.

"I stood out there with him day after day," recalled Henrich. "Mickey had a tough time making the adjustment from shortstop to the outfield, because there were so many things he had to learn that were unnatural to him.

UPI/Bettmann Newsphotos

"We must have hit hundreds of fly balls to him while I tried to teach him the finer points of playing the outfield. I had to teach him how to use sunglasses. Knowing when to flip them down as the ball comes out of the shadows can be pretty tricky. Mickey had never used them before, and I thought he never would get the hang of them. Finally, I figured he had it nailed down."

Not quite.

The first spring training game was against the Cleveland Indians, and Stengel started the excited rookie in center field. In his autobiography, *The Mick,* Mantle recalled what happened next:

"Practice makes perfect, right? . . . My first game as a Yankee. And Cleveland shortstop Ray Boone hit a line drive straight at me. I ran in a few steps and flipped my sunglasses down. *Bam!* Nothing but blackness. The ball caught me square on the forehead."

Left fielder Gene Woodling dashed over, grabbed the ball, and threw it in. He then ran to Mantle's side and, with great concern in his voice, asked not about Mickey's head, but, "Did the glasses break?"

Meanwhile, in the dugout, Henrich threw up his hands in despair. "Oh, no, back to the drawing board," he moaned.

Trainer Gus Mauch ran out to the injured rookie, applied cold compresses to the rising knot on Mantle's head, and led him off the field. As he staggered into the dugout, Mickey looked over at his new teammates. "Everybody was laughing," he recalled. "After that, I had nowhere to go except up."

Wade Boggs

Third Baseman • Boston, A.L. • June 25, 1982

Superstar Wade Boggs suffered his most mortifying moment in the major leagues during his first important game, when his team was really counting on him.

As a rookie for the Boston Red Sox in 1982, the then 25-year-old third baseman showed great potential with a .318 minor league batting average. But he couldn't crack into the starting lineup because Boston's third sacker at the time was Carney Lansford, the defending American League batting champion.

For nearly three months Boggs spent most of his time on the bench, wondering when he'd get the opportunity to show what he could do. But then, with the Red Sox in the thick of a pennant race, Lansford broke his ankle. Now it was up to Wade to fill in for the team's best player.

Boggs was thrust into the starting lineup on the opening game of the biggest series of the season up to that time. The front-running Red Sox were playing host to the second-place Milwaukee Brewers at sold-out Fenway Park. Wade confidently announced he was ready and not the least bit nervous. Still, everyone wondered if the rookie could handle the challenge, and when the Red Sox took the field, all eyes were on Wade Boggs.

At first he wished all those eyes had been shut.

In the biggest game of his life, Wade booted the first ball hit to him in the first inning for an error. Fans began to roll their eyes and groan. Then, in the same frame, Boggs mishandled the second ball grounded to him for another miscue. Now the fans began to boo and count the days when Lansford would return.

"It was a little disastrous," Wade recalled. "There was a considerable amount of pressure from all the fans and the press, wondering if I could do as well as Carney did. I guess I was more nervous than I thought.

"I was just hoping the inning would get over. Wouldn't you know that I got another grounder hit to me. This time, I fielded it cleanly and threw to [second baseman] Jerry Remy for the force-out. The fans then gave me a standing ovation."

It was a derisive cheer, as the unforgiving Boston fans let the chagrined rookie know they were none too pleased with his performance or the two gift runs he helped give the Brewers (who wound up winning 9–3).

"When I came into the dugout," said Boggs, "[veteran teammate] Dwight Evans patted me on the rear and said, 'Don't worry about it—everybody has those days.' It's just that mine came in the first inning of a big game."

Walking Scared

New York Yankees shortstop Bill Werber made his major league debut in 1930 in front of a packed Yankee Stadium. The 22-year-old rookie had never seen so many people together in his entire life, and was shaking like a leaf.

In his first time at bat he managed to draw a walk. At the end of the inning veteran second baseman Tony Lazzeri patted him on the back and said, "Good work, kid. You've got a good eye."

"Good eye?" said Werber with a chuckle. "I was just too doggone scared to take that bat off my shoulder!"

Bret Saberhagen

Pitcher • Kansas City, A.L. • April 4, 1984

The most embarrassing pitch that Cy Young Award winner Bret Saberhagen ever threw was his very first pitch in the major leagues.

Saberhagen was a scared 19-year-old rookie when he was summoned from the bullpen in relief of Kansas City Royals starter Paul Splittorff in a 1984 game against the New York Yankees. Royals manager Dick Howser handed Saberhagen the ball and said,"Don't worry about the runner on first. He's not very fast and I don't think he'll be stealing. Just concentrate on the batter."

Bret, trying hard to hide his nervousness, threw his warm-up pitches, then took a deep breath and prepared to hurl his first major league pitch. He stared at his catcher, Don Slaught, for the sign.

"Slaught put down the pitchout sign, which was his index finger and his little finger put together," recalled Saberhagen. "A pitchout was the farthest thing from my mind because Howser had told me not to worry about the runner. So all I saw were two fingers, the sign for a curveball."

Bret went into his stretch and then threw a curve—in more ways than one. As soon as Saberhagen released the ball, Slaught jumped outside, expecting to catch the pitchout. Instead, the ball broke sharply over the outside corner of the plate for a called strike. Then, after barely missing the plate umpire, the pitch sailed all the way to the backstop as the runner scooted to second base.

Saberhagen knew immediately that he had screwed up. "I thought, 'Oh, boy, there're a lot of people in the stands laughing right now.' Here I was trying to impress people, and look what happened on my first major league pitch."

Third baseman George Brett realized that Saberhagen had crossed up the catcher. "It wasn't funny at the time, but it's funny as hell now," said Brett. "Here was this skinny 19-year-old kid scared to death, and his first pitch goes right across the plate and back to the screen. It made you wonder what he was going to do next."

Added second baseman Frank White, "The first thing I thought of was, 'What a way to start a career.' "

Look Out Below

In his major league debut in 1965, American League umpire Marty Springstead had to contend with Frank Howard, the Washington Senators' mammoth six-foot, seven-inch, 250-pound outfielder.

Springstead, calling balls and strikes, was more than a little nervous. During Howard's first at-bat, the rookie ump called the first pitch around the knees a strike. Howard turned around and bellowed, "Get something straight, buster. I don't know where you came from or what you're doing in the major leagues, but they don't call a strike on me with that pitch. Understand?"

Howard dug into the batter's box and took the next pitch around the knees.

"Two!" hollered Springstead confidently.

Howard wheeled around and glowered. "Two what?"

"Too low, Frank," the ump said meekly. "It was much too low."

Pat Tabler

Second Baseman • Chicago, N.L. • Aug. 21, 1981

The only thing Pat Tabler needed to make his big league debut complete was a deep dark hole to crawl into and hide.

"They don't have any holes in the middle of the infield at Wrigley Field, but I sure was looking for one," recalled Tabler. "It was the most embarrassing predicament I'd ever been in. I just wanted to disappear. I even prayed for a tornado to come down and get me out of there."

When Tabler took the field for the first time, it was the fulfillment of a lifelong dream to make it to the majors.

The Chicago Cubs front office publicly touted Tabler as "the second baseman of the future." But in his debut game against the visiting San Francisco Giants, Tabler soon looked like just another member of the same old sorry Cubs who had kept the faithful in tears for years.

His mental blunder lost the game for the Cubs.

"When I started the game, I was so excited I couldn't concentrate," Tabler recalled. "I had to keep pinching myself to realize I was really playing in Wrigley Field. I even got a hit my first time up in the big leagues, and I thought, 'Oh, wow! This is awesome!' I was just going through the motions because I was practically in shock. I didn't know the number of outs, the inning, or even the score."

And that was the problem.

In the top of the eighth inning with the score tied at 3–3, the Giants loaded the bases with one out. Pinch hitter Jim Wolford then tapped a double-play ball to shortstop Ivan DeJesus, who scooped it up and tossed it to Tabler. It should have been a textbook double play. But apparently Tabler forgot to read the book.

He grabbed the toss and stepped on the bag for the force-out at second. But he didn't pivot and throw to first to record his first major league double play. Instead, Tabler kept the ball and ran toward the Cubs third base dugout—while the winning run scampered across the plate!

"I knew I had screwed up when [Cubs third baseman] Kenny Reitz came running at me, screaming, 'No! No! No!' " said Tabler. "Then it hit me. There were only two outs! I started to throw to first, pretending that I really knew what I was doing, but it was much too late. I felt like I'd been caught naked out there in front of all those people. The only bright spot was that it wasn't on national television."

Because of that gift run, the Cubs lost the game 4–3. "When I came into the clubhouse, all the writers were there in front of my locker waiting for me," said Tabler. "I knew then that I really was in the big leagues."

Time to Chuck It

Before Chuck Connors became a TV star of such hits as "The Rifleman" and "Branded," he was trying to make it as a major league ball player.

But Connors just wasn't good enough—and he knew it. In 1949, his first

year in the bigs, he got to bat only one time as a member of the Brooklyn Dodgers.

In his debut Connors grounded into a double play. After getting thrown out at first, he kept right on running—straight for the clubhouse.

"Hey, where do you think you're going?" shouted first base coach Jake Pitler.

Alluding to the Dodgers farm team, Connors replied from over his shoulder, "To Montreal." And that's exactly where the team sent him.

Jack Onslow

Catcher • New York, N.L. • Sept. 3, 1917

Rookie catcher Jack Onslow was ejected from a game before he had a chance to catch a single pitch.

Actually, the only thing Onslow caught was hell from the umpire following an argument instigated by opposing batter and troublemaker Rabbit Maranville.

Onslow, who played a few games for the Detroit Tigers in 1912, spent the next five years in the minors before the New York Giants called him up at the tail end of the 1917 season.

In the seventh inning of a game against the Boston Braves, Onslow went in to catch as Maranville stepped up to the plate. When Onslow put on his mask and settled into his crouch behind home plate, the mischievous Rabbit thought he'd have a little fun at the rookie's expense. The veteran wise guy turned to plate umpire Bill Klem, pointed to Onslow, and asked the ump, "Who is this guy?"

"I don't know," answered Klem. Then tapping Onslow on the shoulder, he said, "Who are you?"

"My name is Onslow," said the catcher.

"Where did you catch before?" Maranville asked.

"For the Tigers," came the reply.

"Oh, I see," said Rabbit. "Up from the minors." He and Klem began to laugh at the crack.

Meanwhile, Onslow was getting hot under the collar. "I don't think that's funny," the rookie said between clenched teeth. "How about we stick to baseball and get on with the game."

But Maranville, thoroughly enjoying this bit of hazing, wouldn't let up. So with a wink, he asked Klem, "What did he say his name is?"

"Onslow," said Klem.

"How does he spell it?"

"I don't know," said the ump. Tapping Onslow on the shoulder again, Klem asked, "How do you spell it?"

By now Onslow was boiling mad, and then finally blew up. He reared up, wheeled around to Klem and roared, "What difference does it make? I'm here to catch a ball game and not be in a silly spelling bee. Let's get going!"

Nobody ever talked that way to the mighty Bill Klem and got away with it. Whipping off his mask, the ump shouted, "Why, you fresh busher, you're out of the game! Now get going!"

So Onslow shuffled off back to the dugout. As he turned around, he saw Maranville laughing his fool head off.

Montreal Expos

1969

To the Montreal faithful, they were Les Expos. To the rest of the baseball world, they were Les Miserables.

As a first-year expansion team, the Montreal Expos proved they were almost as bad as the 1962 Mets—and in some cases they were worse. Although the Expos lost "only" 110 games compared to the record-setting 120 losses by the Amazin' Mets, Montreal set a new mark for the longest losing streak of an expansion team, with 20 straight setbacks. The old record had belonged to New York, with 17.

The Expos looked funny from the day they first put on their uniforms. After seeing Montreal's red, white, and blue caps with the sections cut like pieces of pie, Mets outfielder Ron Swoboda asked, "Where are their propellers?"

On Opening Day the Expos raced out to a 3–0 lead, then blew it with five errors in one inning. Still, they managed to win 8–7. From then on Montreal lived up to expectations. The team wasn't supposed to win many games—and it didn't.

Wrote sportswriter Bob Verdi, "Les Expos had a curious collection of players, made curiouser by the fact that their pitchers were lanceurs, their batters frappeurs, and their outfielders voltigeurs. But translated into either English or French, this was a club that couldn't even clear customs without committing an error."

Montreal third baseman Coco Laboy became an early cult hero. His specialty was the "daily double." More than once on a routine grounder, he kicked the ball, then when he tried again to pick it up, he kicked the glove off his hand.

Shortstop Bobby Wine led the entire National League East in errors with 31—and in bruises from mishandled balls bouncing off his shins, wrists, and chest.

First baseman Ron Fairly had a habit of losing sight of balls thrown from fellow infielders, because, he said, he was blinded by the sun setting behind third. Fairly, who began wearing sunglasses in the early innings of home night games because of the bothersome sunset, told his infielders that they'd be better off rolling the ball to him.

The pitchers owned a patent on wildness. In a doubleheader with the San Francisco Giants, the Expos walked 19 batters. The next night they issued another 11 passes. This inspired hurler Joe Sparma. Expos Manager Gene Mauch instructed him to issue an intentional walk with opposing runners on second and third. Now how hard could that be? Very. During the free pass, he uncorked a pitch so wild that both runners scored.

Midway through the season the Expos, looking for experience, picked up reliever Dick "The Monster" Radatz, a huge right-hander with a penchant to party. He brought along the experience, but left behind his fastball. Radatz didn't win a game in his 22 appearances and quickly fell out of favor with Mauch. One evening in Atlanta an attendant mistakenly dumped a wheelbarrow full of crushed ice on the steps of the Montreal dugout. When asked what happened, Mauch replied sarcastically, "Nothing. Radatz just spilled his cocktail."

The highlight of the Expos season was the record 20-game losing streak. Everyone did his share. The lanceurs helped out with timely wild pitches and ninth-inning gopher balls. The voltigeurs missed fly balls while scoreboard watching, and threw to bases where no one was covering—and where runners had already passed. The frappeurs, with bats as cold as the Canadian winter, excelled in clutch whiffs and game-losing double-play grounders.

Within an hour after the historic 20th loss, a man of the cloth made the rounds in the clubhouse. He approached Mauch and said, "I've been talking to the boys and they've shown me the team may be down, but it hasn't quit."

"How's that?" the manager asked.

"The players asked for a blessing—not last rites," replied the clergyman with a straight face.

The next night the Expos beat the Dodgers 4–3 to snap the skid and win for the first time in over four weeks. "I feel I've shaken a bad habit," said Mauch. "I don't know how much more I could have stood. I'm getting older, you know." There was no champagne in the clubhouse because, as bullpen coach Jerry Zimmerman said, "How can you get excited about winning one and losing 20?"

Shameful Debut Moments

1987—The Cincinnati Reds called up Pat Pacillo from the Nashville farm team with plans to pitch him immediately. After a 4½-hour drive from Nashville, Pacillo pulled into the Riverfront Stadium garage in the first inning, but he couldn't park there because the attendant refused to believe Pacillo played for the Reds. So Pacillo had to park his car three miles away and walk back, arriving in the fourth inning. The rookie then worked five innings in his debut, giving up two runs and five hits in a 3–2 loss to the Pittsburgh Pirates.

1981—The Atlanta Braves had already taken the field as pitcher Steve Bedrosian lingered in the dugout, psyching himself up for his first major league start. Then he ran up the dugout steps, smashed right into the railing, bruised his forearm, and swallowed his tobacco. He was sick and hurting the rest of the game.

1980—In his debut, Philadelphia Phillies hurler Bob Walk (shown in photo) got caught off guard when it was his turn to bat. Having just come up from the minors, where the designated hitter was used, Walk didn't quite know what to do. He forgot to go to the on-deck circle until he was ordered there. Then, after swinging a leaded bat, he dropped it—and walked up to the plate without any bat at all! "I pulled a U-turn and went back to the dugout for a bat," Walk recalled. "From then on I was known as a space case."

1962—In his first time at bat, Andy Etchebarren of the Baltimore Orioles complained to plate umpire Ed Runge on a couple of called strikes. "Son," said the ump. "Look around these stands. You see all these people? They didn't come here to see you watch the pitches. You better start swinging the bat." Etchebarren did—and struck out.

1928—In his debut as a starting pitcher for the Philadelphia Phillies, Marty Walker faced just five batters. He gave up two hits and three walks before he was yanked. He calmly strode off the mound, quietly took his shower, and was never seen in the major leagues again.

Lefty Gomez

Pitcher • New York, A.L. • April–July, 1930

In his debut year, Hall of Famer Lefty Gomez planned on making a big name for himself. Instead, he made a big fool out of himself.

When Gomez broke in as a 20-year-old rookie with the New York Yankees in 1930, he was relegated to the bullpen, where he waited impatiently to pitch in his first game.

One day, three weeks into the season, Lefty was in the bullpen watching future Hall of Famer Herb Pennock pitch. Pennock, the only other left-handed hurler on the Yankees, was twirling a fine game into the eighth inning. Suddenly, a line drive tore through Pennock's glove and caromed off his knee for a hit to load the bases. The hurler limped painfully around the mound as manager Bob Shawkey motioned to the bullpen for Gomez.

The call Lefty had yearned for had finally come!

"I was frightened to death walking in," recalled Gomez, "but I thought I'd cover it up by acting big. I nonchalantly hopped the bullpen fence and walked to the mound. Wanting to appear alert, I told Shawkey, 'Bags loaded, one out, we have a one-run lead, and I need to keep the ball low for the double play.' Shawkey looked at me kind of funny and said, 'Pennock broke the webbing of his glove. Just give him your mitt and go back to the bullpen.' "

The following week Gomez finally got into his first big league game against the Washington Senators. As Lefty peered at the catcher for the sign, the butterflies in his stomach were so thick that he temporarily lost his concentration. His catcher, Bill Dickey, called for a fastball. Gomez nodded and then threw a beautiful curve that zoomed right past the crossed-up catcher.

Dickey walked to the mound, patted Lefty on the back, and said, "Look, kid, there's nothing to be nervous about. It's just the same as pitching in the minors—only up here the catcher is supposed to know what's coming."

Gomez gave up two runs on four hits in four innings and lost the game. About three weeks later he was scheduled to start against the Boston Red Sox in tiny Fenway Park.

Half an hour before game time Shawkey found Lefty standing in a telephone booth just outside the Yankee clubhouse. "What are you doing in there?" the manager demanded. "Why aren't you out on the field getting warmed up?"

"I think I'll stay in here until it's time to pitch," said the rookie. "That way, when I'm on the mound, the park will seem bigger to me." That day he gave up four runs in seven innings but didn't figure in the decision.

Lefty then lost four games in a row. At the end of July, Gomez, sporting a 2–5 record and a hefty 5.55 ERA, was sent back to the minors. Before going, he told the press, "I get by all right until I begin throwing my gopher ball— it'll go for two bases sometimes. Other times it'll go for three or four bases. When that happens, I go for the showers."

Cotton Pippen

Pitcher • St. Louis, N.L. • Sept. 13, 1936

Cotton Pippen's debut on the base paths was so shameful, he turned a double into a double play.

The St. Louis Cardinals rookie hurler was making only his second major league appearance, in a game against the New York Giants. In the third inning the Cardinals' Brusie Ogrodowski led off with a single. Up to the plate stepped Pippen, batting for the first time in the big leagues. His knees shook from the jitters as he tried to bunt the runner to second. But he fouled off two pitches. Then Pippen tapped weakly to second baseman Burgess White-head, who flipped the ball to shortstop Dick Bartell for the intended force-out. But Bartell dropped the ball and both runners were safe.

Pippen's heart was pounding. Here he was, on first base for the very first time in front of a standing room only crowd of 67,000 at the Polo Grounds. The two teams were locked in a tight pennant race and every game seemed a matter of life and death. Pippen knew he couldn't afford to screw up now. He had to run the bases smartly.

The next hitter, Terry Moore, socked a single to right field, scoring Ogrodowski. Pippen cautiously held up at second. Batter Art Garibaldi then sent a tremendous poke over the head of right fielder Mel Ott for extra bases. But Pippen—being extra cautious so he wouldn't make a mistake—screwed up anyway. He didn't move from second base until he saw the ball bounce off the outfield wall. Then he motored around third and headed for the plate.

Meanwhile, Moore, who saw immediately that Garibaldi's smash was a clean hit, took off from first and tore around the bases. To Moore's surprise, he nearly ran up the back of the late-breaking Pippen right after both had rounded third. So Moore turned around and went back to third.

By now the relay throw to catcher Gus Mancuso had Pippen so badly beaten that the rookie made an about-face and backtracked to third. Seeing this, Moore retreated and tried to return to second, but he was caught in a rundown. So Pippen, trying to atone for the mess he had caused, dashed for home once again, only to fall flat on his face. Mancuso called for the ball and ran up the line to tag out the prone rookie.

Then the catcher fired the ball to Bartell, who tagged out Moore as he slid back into second. Garibaldi, who had been on second, now hightailed it back toward first. Bartell fired the ball to first baseman Bill Terry, but Garibaldi beat the throw by an eyelash. Otherwise, Garibaldi would have doubled into a triple play—courtesy of Cotton Pippen.

In the dugout, Cardinals manager Frankie Frisch fell off the bench with a bad case of apoplexy. He jumped all over the red-faced rookie. "Since you can't find your way around the bases," shouted Frisch, "let's see if you can find your way to the showers! Now get out of here!"

The Cardinals lost 8–4. It was Pippen's first and last season with St. Louis.

Ray Boggs

Pitcher • Boston, N.L. • Sept. 17, 1928

In one of the wildest pitching debuts in the major leagues, Ray Boggs went Cub hunting—and bagged three of them in one inning.

"It seemed like I hit just about everybody in the park except the grounds-keeper," recalled the chagrined hurler.

Boggs, then 24, had joined the Boston Braves only days before his embarrassing debut against the Chicago Cubs. He had been playing pickup games in Wyoming, where he developed a mean sidearm curveball. A friend of Braves player-manager Rogers Hornsby suggested that Boggs be given a tryout. With the Braves mired in last place, Hornsby decided he had nothing to lose, so he brought Boggs to Beantown.

When Boggs saw that major league pitchers threw overhanded, he quit throwing sidearm and lost his control. He had yet to find it as he warmed up in the bullpen during a game in which the Cubs were clubbing the Braves 14–1.

"I'd never seen hitting like that in my life and I was scared to death," Boggs recalled. "In the top of the ninth Hornsby sent me in to pitch. He felt that since we were getting beat so badly, I couldn't do any more damage."

Hornsby was wrong. Boggs did plenty of damage—mainly to the bodies of the Cubs who faced the wild rookie.

The first victim was Woody English, who wasn't quick enough to dodge out of the way of an errant inside pitch. He limped down to first rubbing the back of his thigh. English hardly had time to take his lead before scooting to second on a wild pitch that sailed over the catcher's head.

English was still trying to catch his breath when Boggs uncorked another wild pitch. Already worn out from running around the bases all afternoon, English halfheartedly trotted toward third and let himself get tagged out.

Meanwhile, Kiki Cuyler stood at the plate and grew more nervous by the second as Boggs's pitches zipped over and behind him like flying shrapnel. Finally he was plunked in the ribs with a pitch. Then, with Hack Wilson at bat, Boggs fired his third wild pitch of the inning, putting Cuyler on second. Wilson never had a chance to swing his dangerous bat because Boggs walked him on four straight pitches.

Riggs Stephenson, the next batter due up, begged Cubs manager Joe McCarthy to send up a pinch hitter. McCarthy refused, saying, "Get up there and take it like a man."

Riggs did as he was told. He took Boggs's next pitch—square in the middle of his butt.

Now, with the bases loaded, Charlie Grimm crept up to the plate and stood as far back in the box as he could and still be in the ballpark. From that distance he reached out and swatted an outside fastball for a single that scored Cuyler. Wilson, looking to help end the inning, strolled toward home and let himself get tagged out.

Somehow the jittery Boggs got the next batter to ground out. The cheers Boggs heard were not from the fans but from the other Cubs, who were dreading batting against him.

For the record, in his first inning as a major leaguer, Boggs hit three batters, flung three wild pitches, walked one, and gave up a run and a hit.

As he walked off the mound, Boggs was consoled by Braves first baseman George Sisler, who told the shell-shocked rookie, "Don't worry. They only got one run off you."

THE BLIGHTS OF SPRING

◆

*Spring training is a time when players are supposed to work out all
the winter kinks and fine-tune their baseball skills. But six weeks in
the warmth of Florida or the Southwest doesn't seem to help some
guys. For them, getting into shape is a question of mind over matter.
They don't mind goofing off, so it doesn't matter how silly they act
in the preseason. For "The Most Foolish Behavior in Spring Training,"
The Baseball Hall of SHAME inducts the following:*

Kirby Puckett

Outfielder • Minnesota, A.L. • Feb. 22, 1987

Kirby Puckett was having such an easy time blasting balls out of the park
during batting practice that it seemed criminal. It nearly was. A policeman
threatened Puckett with arrest if he didn't stop hitting.

The cop put the cuffs on Kirby's batting practice at Tinker Field, the
Minnesota Twins spring training facility in Orlando, Florida. The All-Star
slugger had hammered about seven balls over the left-field fence when all of
a sudden a policeman and an angry, shirtless, long-haired man climbed over
the outfield wall and ran toward home plate.

It was then that Puckett learned he would have been better off if he were a
singles hitter. His out-of-the-park shots were landing in a parking area for
people attending a tractor pull at the neighboring Orlando Stadium. One ball
shattered a windshield, nearly spraying glass on the wife of the shirtless man,
and a few other balls dented some parked trucks, prompting the police
action.

Sergeant Robert Newsome of the Orlando Police Department marched up
to Tom Mee, the club's media relations director, and told him, "You have to
stop this batting practice right now."

"This is serious training," replied Mee. "We have to maximize our time. We can't just stop like that."

"These people [in the parking lot] have been parked there for three days," said Sergeant Newsome.

"Maybe so. But we've been here since 1936," said Mee.

Then Sergeant Newsome pointed to Puckett and told Mee, "I'm going to tell that man to stop batting, and if he doesn't, I'm going to arrest him."

The cop went up to Puckett and shouted, "Hey! Hey! Hey! If you swing that bat one more time, you're going to jail!"

"Man, I'm just hitting the ball, doing my job," said the startled player. "I don't want to go to jail." Puckett wisely stopped swinging. Twins executive vice president Andy McPhail had the workout continue in a covered cage by the bullpen, thus averting Puckett's arrest.

"Do you believe this?" an incredulous Puckett said to reporters. "The cop makes me stop hitting just when I was getting in a groove."

Joked McPhail: "If Kirby had been arrested, it might have been the best thing that ever happened to tourism in Orlando. Can you imagine all the Minnesotans descending on this place chanting, 'Release Kirby Puckett! Release Kirby Puckett!' "

Wilbert Robinson

Manager • Brooklyn, N.L. • March, 1915

Wilbert Robinson tried catching a baseball dropped from an airplane and wound up catching a lot of good-natured flak.

During spring training in 1915, Uncle Robbie—as the Brooklyn manager was fondly called—was listening to some of his players talk about the remarkable feat of Washington Senators catcher Gabby Street. A few years earlier, Street had caught a ball dropped from atop the Washington Monument.

Robinson, a former catcher himself with the old Baltimore Orioles, took this as a personal challenge. "Hell, that's nothing," said the roly-poly manager. "I can catch a ball that's dropped from an airplane."

Team trainer Jack Coombs, a wizard with figures, calculated the velocity and force of a baseball dropped from the height of several hundred feet. He said it seemed a little dangerous, but Robinson scoffed at him. Uncle Robbie was determined to be the first to accomplish this feat for the aviation and baseball worlds.

So Coombs climbed into a biplane in the lone seat behind pioneer woman flyer Ruth Law. Before they took off, however, Dodger outfielder Casey Stengel ran up to the plane. Whether out of concern for Uncle Robbie's safety or out of a lust for laughs, Casey substituted a grapefruit for the baseball.

The plane took off and circled several hundred feet above the Dodgers training camp. Finally the signal was given and Coombs dropped the grapefruit.

The five-foot, eight-inch, 230-pound former catcher saw the "ball" leave the airplane, so he waved everybody away like an outfielder and shouted, "I've got it! I've got it!" The plummeting sphere looked bigger and bigger to him as it sped earthward. Bravely camped under the grapefruit, Robinson, who still thought it was a baseball, was ready to make the historic catch.

The grapefruit slammed into his glove with a loud splat as seeds, juice, and pieces of fruit splattered all over him. The impact tore the glove off his hand and flipped him right over on his back.

Uncle Robbie lay there looking like a ghost. The Dodgers rushed to his aid, but once they saw he wasn't hurt, they burst out laughing. All but Robinson, that is. He was burned up because he had risked life and limb over a lousy grapefruit instead of an official baseball.

"I'd have caught it," he said, "except for that damn cloudburst of grapefruit juice."

Double the Fun

In a 1933 spring training game, Ripper Collins of the St. Louis Cardinals was called on to pinch-hit.

Before leaving the dugout, he tucked a ball under his left arm where nobody could see it, including plate umpire Bill Klem.

On the first pitch, Collins dragged a bunt toward first and at the same time let the ball pop out from under his arm.

"The pitcher ran over to get the ball that I had bunted and the catcher picked up the one I had dropped," Collins recalled. "Neither one threw, they were so surprised.

"Klem threw me out of the game. He told me, 'There will be none of that, young man. This is serious business, even in an exhibition game.'

"For a minute, though, it was fun."

Casey Stengel

Outfielder • Brooklyn, N.L. • March, 1912

In one of the zaniest capers ever seen during a spring training game, Casey Stengel literally popped out of the ground to catch a fly ball.

Long before he became a veteran outfielder and Hall of Fame manager, Stengel was a young, fun-loving prospect for the Brooklyn Dodgers. He first showed his flair for comedy in a spring training game in 1912.

At the start of an exhibition game in Pensacola, Florida, Casey trotted out to left field, where he noticed a sunken box containing the water-pipe connections for the field's sprinkling system.

At first he paid little attention to the box and its metal cover. But as the game dragged on with his team far out in front, Stengel's wacky mind went to work. As he took his position to start the seventh inning, he lifted up the heavy lid and crawled down inside the sunken box. No one paid any attention since all eyes were on the pitcher and batter.

From the dugout and from the stands, Casey couldn't be seen, but he was able to lift the lid and peek over the edge of the sunken box and watch the action. He saw the first two men ground out. As luck would have it, the next batter lifted a high, lazy fly ball that was headed for a spot about 15 feet from where Casey was hiding. The crowd followed the flight of the ball and then looked to see where Stengel was positioned. Suddenly the fans gasped in bewilderment—there was nobody in left field!

Meanwhile, Casey was biding his time. He planned to leap out of the sunken box at the right moment and make the catch, as if he had been in position the whole time.

But Stengel hadn't factored in one important thing—the metal cover was heavier than he had figured. Although he managed to raise it over his head, he wasn't able to lift it high enough to allow him to scramble out onto the field. But Lady Luck—who obviously had a sense of humor—came to the rescue. While Casey was struggling with the cover, a gust of wind blew the ball over toward the box.

So with one hand holding up the cover, Stengel stuck out his gloved hand and caught the ball! It was probably the most unusual putout ever entered in a "box" score.

Another of Casey's classic capers occurred during a spring training game in Fort Wayne, Indiana, in 1920 when he was a new member of the Philadelphia Phillies.

Stengel failed to appear at the clubhouse and was not on the field when the game started. Instead, he sat in the stands dressed as a Hoosier farmer.

Shortly after the game got under way, Casey began to heckle the big leaguers. "You city slickers ain't so good!" he yelled from the stands. "You can't hit a lick! Why, I can hit better than any of you!" The fans—believing Stengel was one of their own Indiana boys—took up his battle cry.

Eventually one of the Phillies became so irritated he approached the stands and confronted the "farmer." Only then did the player realize it was Casey, but he didn't let on that he knew.

Instead, the player challenged the "farmer" and said, "Well, if you think you're so good, you try it."

"You're darn right I will," said Casey. "I'll show you!" The crowd went wild as the Phillies "loaned" him a pair of baseball shoes. Going to bat in his blue-denim coveralls, Stengel faced the Philly pitcher, who deliberately grooved a fastball. To the delirious joy of the Fort Wayne fans, their farmer hit a home run over the right-field fence. The crowd continued to cheer themselves hoarse as the Phillies "loaned" him a glove and let him play in right field so he could prove he was just as good as the city slickers.

The fans that day never realized they were watching Casey Stengel at his entertaining best.

Billy Martin

Second Baseman • New York, A.L. • March, 1952

Spring training in 1952 turned into spring straining for Billy Martin. He broke his ankle while demonstrating how to slide for the TV cameras.

It happened at the New York Yankees training camp in St. Petersburg, Florida, where the recently retired Joe DiMaggio showed up with a camera crew. DiMaggio, who was launching a new career in television, was the on-air talent for a show sponsored by a macaroni company. He wanted to take some films of his former teammates in action and asked Martin to show viewers how to slide.

Billy was only too happy to oblige, since the film was for his old friend. With the cameras rolling, Martin raced to second and dove headfirst. On his next attempt he made a nifty hook slide. Then Billy put everything he had in his third slide. He dashed to second, hit the dirt, and . . . crack! He rolled along the ground writhing in pain.

DiMaggio watched in horror. He knew what it was to suffer pain. It was at this very camp, years earlier, that Joe fell asleep under a sun lamp and was burned so badly that he required hospital treatment.

Billy was rushed to the hospital, where X rays revealed his ankle was broken in two places. Martin spent the rest of spring training on crutches.

Yankees manager Casey Stengel was so unnerved by this accident that he went overboard trying to protect the rest of his players.

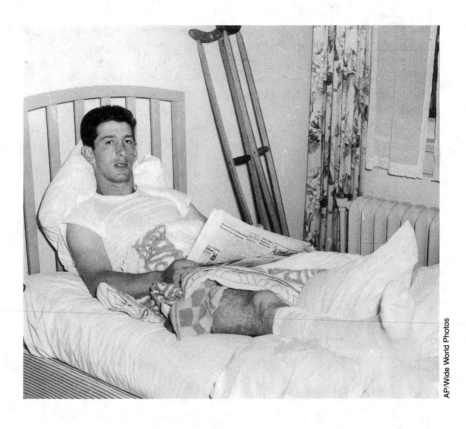

The day after Martin's mishap, a reporter for a national magazine asked Stengel for permission to have outfielder Jackie Jensen excused from practice so a photographer could take poolside pictures of Jensen with his wife and daughter.

"You know what happened to that boy Martin yesterday, don't you?" asked Stengel, who then proceeded to answer his own question. "Broke his ankle, that's what he did. Now, supposing this boy Jackie drowns? Is your magazine going to give me somebody to play the outfield in place of him? That spaghetti company [DiMaggio's sponsor] ain't sending me any second basemen."

A Message for Canseco

Oakland Athletics star José Canseco didn't show up early for spring training like the rest of the starters did in 1988 because he was attending baseball-card shows in Pennsylvania and New York.

His absence didn't sit too well with his teammates. They let him know how they felt—in a fun way.

At the end of a team meeting, a sheet was removed from a large table in front of the players. On the table were several José Canseco model bats, José Canseco buttons, and a large poster of the slugger.

A hand-printed sign read, "Welcome to José Canseco Autograph Day. Appearing for the first time: José Canseco. 10 A.M. to 2 P.M. Evening Lecture. Concepts of Team Play. Special Guest Speaker: José (Card Show) Canseco."

Dazzy Vance   Jacques Fournier   Hank DeBerry

Pitcher   **First Baseman**   **Catcher**

Brooklyn, N.L. • March, 1925

Three daffy Dodgers conspired to pull off a ruse that hoodwinked both the batter and the umpire during a spring training game in 1925.

The Dodgers were playing an exhibition game against the Southern Association's team from Montgomery, Alabama, when Brooklyn's fireball king Dazzy Vance conjured up a wacky play he later said was the funniest he ever staged on the diamond.

It had to do with a direct violation of the rule that prohibits a hurler from making any motion to pitch without having the ball in his possession.

With a couple of Montgomery runners on base, two out, and the count 3-and-2 on the batter, Vance summoned first baseman Jacques Fournier to the mound. Dazzy explained his plan and then, under cover of a deep conference, slipped the ball into Fournier's glove.

The two returned to their positions. Vance then went into his stretch and went through the motions of putting everything he had on his next pitch. As the Dazzler cut loose, Fournier, standing off first base, rifled the ball to the plate. It landed smack into catcher Hank DeBerry's glove with a loud thud. The batter blinked. So did the umpire.

Finally the umpire shook his head and said, "Sorry, boy, but that one was even too fast for me to see. I'll have to call it a strike . . . and you're out!"

Vance said later that the real hero of this caper was DeBerry, who was an unwitting accomplice. "Jacques and I had forgotten all about letting Hank in on the secret, so he was as much in the dark as either the batter or the umpire. But by that time Hank had been with me long enough not to be taken by surprise, no matter what I did."

Dizzy Trout

Pitcher • Detroit, A.L. • March 1937

As a rookie pitcher, Dizzy Trout figured he needed more than a strong right arm to gain attention in spring training. He needed a gimmick. So he deliberately acted like a screwball. It almost worked, until his temper got in the way.

Before becoming a star pitcher for the Detroit Tigers during the 1940s, Dizzy was the biggest hit and biggest flop in the spring of 1937.

At the time, Trout idolized St. Louis Cardinals pitching ace Dizzy Dean, who was at the peak of his career. So Trout adopted the nickname Dizzy before heading to camp. "I figured that if his name was worth forty thousand dollars a year, then it was good enough for me," Trout recalled years later. "I thought that by acting a little screwy I could draw extra customers for the club, furnish copy for the newspapers, and make more money for myself."

When Trout arrived at the Tigers camp in Lakeland, Florida, the 21-year-old country hurler created an instant sensation. First, he explained that although his given name was Paul Howard Trout, he went by the name of Dizzy.

"I got my name when I was pitching for Terre Haute," he told rapt reporters, teammates, and fans. "One day, it started to rain. I thought the dugouts were reserved for club owners, so I looked around and saw an awning in center field. I ran for it. It kept raining harder and I kept running harder. I ran right under that awning before I discovered it was just a sign painted on the outfield fence. I've been a little dizzy ever since." Everyone bought the story.

During exhibition games when he wasn't pitching, Dizzy sat in the stands and spun more yarns like this one: "I was born in Sandcut, Indiana, but don't ask me where in Indiana, because I couldn't tell you. Nobody can tell you. The town's built on sand and some nights you go to bed and the next morning you wake up and the town is a mile or two from where it was the day before. That's because a big wind would come up in the night and move the town."

Trout received more newspaper copy than Tigers stars Hank Greenberg and Charlie Gehringer. He once pitched while standing in a wheelbarrow. Reporters wrote everything about him—even the way he dressed. Dizzy had arrived at camp with two steamer trunks packed with fancy clothes, including a dozen hats and two dozen pairs of shoes. He wore loud socks, loud suspenders, and even louder neckties.

Trout made sure he was the center of attention on the mound. He loved drama. Whenever he got into a jam, he slowly and deliberately pulled a red bandanna from his hip pocket and wiped his sweaty brow. Sometimes he called time with the bases loaded just so he could take a chaw of tobacco out of his pocket and jam it in his cheek.

Because Dizzy chose to start spring training early, he was ahead of both batters and pitchers. He looked great. He was so cocky that in the second week of camp he announced he'd pitch for the Tigers on Opening Day.

Detroit manager Mickey Cochrane was impressed. Although Dizzy's wackiness and boasts sometimes annoyed him, Cochrane had planned to keep the rookie on the roster. But the manager soon began having doubts when Trout revealed a whole other, fiery side of himself.

When Trout begged for the chance to start against Dizzy Dean and the

Cardinals at Daytona Beach, Cochrane consented. So Trout told everyone how he would show up Dean.

Shortly before the game, Trout strolled past the St. Louis bench and said snootily, "Well, how do you hillbillies like wearing shoes?" The Cards stared back at him in stony silence. Once the game began, the St. Louis bench jockeys swung into action and rode him unmercifully.

Trout, listening to his hecklers, mistakenly thought that fans in the stands were riding him. At the end of the first inning he ran up to the backstop and challenged everybody in the stands to come down and duke it out. Hustled by teammates back to the dugout, Dizzy kicked the bats around, pushed over the water cooler, and finished his outburst by throwing his glove into the grandstand. When he went back to the mound for the next inning, the Cardinals shelled him.

Cochrane hoped Trout's temper tantrum was an isolated incident. But in his next appearance, Dizzy threw a fit because he failed to field a grounder. In his blind rage, he grooved every pitch until he blew a Detroit lead and had to be pulled.

During his next appearance, Trout disagreed with the plate umpire on a decision. Dizzy became so enraged that he deliberately walked the next six batters before he was yanked.

Cochrane had seen enough. Back in Lakeland the following day, the Tigers manager was sitting in front of the clubhouse when Dizzy borrowed a motorcycle and began riding it around the outfield. Then he roared over to Cochrane.

"How do you like my motorcycling?" Trout asked.

"You're doing fine," Cochrane said coldly. "Just stay on that thing and head north to Toledo [Detroit's farm team], because that's where you'll be pitching on Opening Day."

It took another two years before Dizzy Trout—the self-made screwball—finally made it to the major leagues.

SNOOZE PLAYS

◆

Major leaguers concentrate on every pitch, every batted ball, every play. Baloney! These guys daydream and get lost in their thoughts just like the rest of us working stiffs. The only problem is that their office is the playing field, and when they get caught napping, they're in for a rude awakening. For "The Most Mind-Boggling Mental Miscues," The Baseball Hall of SHAME inducts the following:

Andre Dawson

Right Fielder • Chicago, N.L. • April 28, 1988

Andre Dawson might be known as "The Hawk," but his most embarrassing moment made him feel like a turkey.

Dawson, the National League's Most Valuable Player in 1987, was at bat for the visiting Chicago Cubs in a game against the San Francisco Giants. With runner Ryne Sandberg on first, Andre lofted a fly ball into short left-center field. But then the tricky winds at Candlestick Park played havoc with the ball.

Shortstop José Uribe ran out while left fielder Jeffrey Leonard and center fielder Brett Butler raced in. At the last second Butler dove for the ball.

To Dawson, who had already rounded first base, it looked like Butler had made the catch. So Andre turned around and, gazing nonchalantly at the ground, trotted back toward the Cubs' third base dugout by way of home plate.

Just as he reached the on-deck circle near the dugout, Dawson sensed that something was wrong. He looked up and saw that his teammates were yelling and waving at him to get back to first. Only then did he realize that the ball had not been caught.

Andre spun on his heels, but before he could make a mad dash back to first base—in fact, before he could even get back to home plate—he was thrown out at first by about 130 feet.

"That was definitely my most embarrassing moment," Dawson recalled. "Here I am almost in the dugout, and they are making the play at first base to get me out.

"I just took for granted that the ball had been caught. I try not to make mental mistakes, but sometimes they happen. When I finally returned to the dugout, I got your basic funny looks and giggles. Well, at least it showed I was human."

Charlie Moore

Catcher • Milwaukee, A.L. • 1973–86

If Lewis Carroll could have seen Charlie Moore play baseball, the famed author probably would have written *Charlie in Blunderland*.

Although considered an otherwise smart catcher for the Milwaukee Brewers, Moore gave new meaning to the term "tools of ignorance." He led the team in boneheaded plays.

Moore suffered his first brain sprain on the final day of the 1973 season, his rookie year. The Brewers led the Boston Red Sox 2–1 in the bottom of the eighth inning at Fenway Park as Milwaukee's Jim Colborn gunned for his 21st win of the year.

But Boston rallied and had runners Tommy Harper on third and Danny Cater at first with one out. Ben Oglivie then lofted a fly ball to center fielder Bob Coluccio, who caught the ball and threw it home. Moore snared the ball and tagged the sliding Harper, but plate umpire Bill Kunkle called the runner safe.

Charlie leaped to his feet and slammed the ball down in a fit of anger. Then he laid into Kunkle with a string of invectives. Unfortunately, Moore never bothered to call time-out and was oblivious to the ball which was now rolling aimlessly toward the Brewers dugout.

Meanwhile, Cater had tagged up from first after the catch and scrambled to second, then to third, and kept on motoring to the plate. Not until Cater crossed home with the winning run did Charlie learn that he had forgotten to call time. The Brewers lost 3–2.

Apparently, Moore didn't learn his lesson. Five years later he committed a similar blunder in another game with the Red Sox, this time in Milwaukee.

In the top of the seventh inning of a 2–2 deadlock, Boston had runners George Scott on second base and Butch Hobson on first with two out. Batter Frank Duffy singled to center fielder Ben Oglivie (who was now with the Brewers). Oglivie fired the ball to Moore, who thought he had the plate blocked, but umpire Rich Garcia called Scott safe.

Moore jumped up and charged Garcia, vigorously protesting the call. But once again Charlie forgot to call time-out. In the heat of the debate, the ball fell out of Moore's glove without him realizing it. Meanwhile, Hobson, who had scooted to third on the hit, kept right on running, crossing the plate unchallenged with the go-ahead run, and Boston won.

Afterward Hobson said, "After I went to third, I saw that Charlie was upset and that he had dropped the ball. That's a live ball. It's still in play. Nobody had called time so I just ran home."

Moore faced the music with the press after the game. "I thought I still had the ball in my glove," he lamented. "The ball must have fallen out when I jumped up to argue with the ump. It was different than the time in 1973. Then, I actually threw the ball down. This time I thought I had the ball." But the results were still the same.

Then there was the time in 1980 when Charlie was struck with another brain spasm that cost his team a victory. In the 11th inning of a tie game, the New York Yankees had loaded the bases with no outs. On a sharp grounder, Brewers third baseman Jim Gantner fielded the ball, stepped on third for the force-out, and fired the ball to Moore at home for what should have been a double play.

Instead of tagging the runner, Charlie merely stepped on the plate, forgetting that his play was not a force-out. Then he decided to throw to first, but the ball popped out of his hand. It didn't matter. The winning run had already slid across the plate.

In the clubhouse after the game, the embarrassed catcher confessed that he forgot the force had been taken off. "All I was thinking about was getting a triple play," he said.

Instead, all Charlie Moore was getting was grief over another misplay.

Strike Two, You're Out!

Andy Van Slyke had trouble counting to two.

When the All-Star outfielder was playing for the St. Louis Cardinals in a 1984 game against the San Diego Padres, he walked away from the plate, thinking he had struck out.

But he only had two strikes on him.

"No one said anything to me until I actually was in the dugout," Van Slyke recalled sheepishly. "Then everyone started screaming at me. The fans got on me good, too, when I walked back out. It was embarrassing, to say the least.

"It wouldn't have been so bad if I had hit a home run. But I struck out on the next pitch. What a waste. I walked all the way up there just to strike out. I should have saved myself a trip."

Keith Hernandez

First Baseman • New York Mets • April 19, 1988

Keith Hernandez could have used a box-seat ticket. On one shameful play, he acted more like a spectator than a New York Mets Gold Glove first baseman.

Along with the 30,000 fans at Shea Stadium, Keith watched aging veteran Mike Schmidt score all the way from first base on a wild pitch. The only difference between Hernandez and the fans was that he could have stopped Schmidt from scoring.

Keith's snooze play occurred in the top of the eighth inning of a home game against the Philadelphia Phillies, who were winning 9–7 at the time.

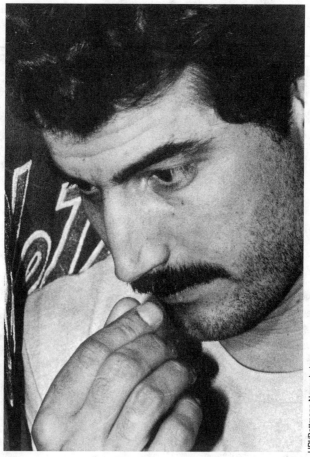

UPI/Bettmann Newsphotos

Schmidt was leading off first with Von Hayes at the plate when Mets pitcher David Cone uncorked a wild pitch.

Cone's fastball bounced in front of the plate and skipped past catcher Gary Carter to the backstop 70 feet away, where it then caromed toward the Phillies third base dugout.

From his position at first base, Hernandez watched Schmidt sprint for second.

Then Hernandez watched Carter and Cone pursue the elusive ball, which by now was skittering along the top steps of the dugout.

Next, Hernandez watched Carter and Cone hover over the ball, waiting for it to go down the steps so that, according to the ground rules, Schmidt could only advance one base. But the ball stayed in the field of play.

And, finally, Hernandez watched Schmidt round third and jog across the plate which had been left unprotected by none other than Keith himself.

"It was incredible," Cone told reporters after the game, which the Mets lost 10–7. "It's not something you work on in spring training—a wild pitch with a man on first."

Hernandez chimed in, "I've never seen anything remotely close to it, ever."

Even so, a Little League first baseman would have known what to do in that situation. "Who should have covered the plate?" manager Dave Johnson asked rhetorically. "The first baseman. It was Keith's responsibility."

It turned out to be Keith's liability.

Babe Young

First Baseman • Cincinnati, N.L. • April 19, 1948

Babe Young flew into such a blind rage that he forgot he was in a baseball game and not a wrestling match. Babe soon found himself not only counted out, but tagged out as well.

In the eighth inning of a game between the Cincinnati Reds and the visiting Pittsburgh Pirates, the Reds were leading 4–1 when Young slapped a ringing double off the right-field fence.

It should have been a stand-up two-bagger. However, eight feet from second base, Pirates shortstop Stan Rojek cut in front of the runner and positioned himself to take the throw from right fielder Dixie Walker. But Babe, with his eyes on the ball, crashed into Rojek and both ended in a heap on the ground. Dazed from the collision, Young crawled the few remaining feet to second base and touched the bag as umpire Jocko Conlan called him safe.

But then Babe forgot all he had learned about the rules. Livid over what he thought was deliberate interference, he leaped off the bag and onto Rojek's back—without bothering to call time-out.

The pair grappled and wrestled in the dust as teammates from both benches charged onto the field. Several fans left their seats and joined the fray. Even the news photographers swarmed onto the field, which only added to the pandemonium and sent the umpires into a frenzy. Plate ump Beans Reardon tried to clear the field. He confronted one cameraman near third base and rapped him over the head with his mask.

"I was right out there in the middle of it all," recalled Hank Sauer, Young's teammate. "We were trying to pull Babe and Stan apart and still keep the photographers off our backs. Everybody was yelling and pushing and going crazy."

Everybody, that is, except Pirates pitcher Vic Lombardi. He picked up the ball that Dixie Walker had thrown in from the outfield. Lombardi then pushed his way through the wild crowd around second base, calmly reached down, and tagged out Babe, who was still scuffling on the ground.

"He never called time-out," Lombardi told Conlan. The umpire agreed and called Young out.

"I guess Babe just got overly excited and forgot what he was doing," said Sauer. "Babe was like that sometimes. We never knew what he was apt to do."

For the Pirates rookie second baseman Monty Basgall, it was a traumatic initiation into major league baseball. "This was my first game, and I didn't know what was going on," he recalled. "All of a sudden, those guys were rolling around in the dirt, punching and cussing each other right in front of me. Then everybody else started running onto the field. It looked like a riot, so I headed for cover. I told myself, 'Hell, if they do this every day, I'm going back to the minors.' "

Bob Skinner

Left Fielder

Bill Virdon

Center Fielder

Pittsburgh, N.L. • June 17, 1959

Pittsburgh Pirates outfielders Bob Skinner and Bill Virdon blew a game simply because they both forgot what inning it was.

Because the two Bucs suffered a bad case of befuddlement, the Chicago Cubs' Cal Neeman huffed and puffed his way to a wacky game-winning "inside-the-cup" home run.

It all happened in the bottom of the eighth inning at Wrigley Field. With the score tied 2–2, the Cubs had runners Ernie Banks at second and Bobby Thomson at first. Up to the plate stepped Neeman, Chicago's 200-pound catcher, not known for either speed or power.

Neeman drilled a sinking liner to left-center field, where Skinner tried for a shoestring catch but failed to snare the ball. As Banks scooted around third and headed for home, Skinner resignedly began jogging toward the Pittsburgh dugout. Somehow, Skinner thought it was the ninth inning and that the game was over when Banks scored.

That an otherwise heads-up veteran like Skinner could make such a mental blunder was hard to believe. Even more unbelievable was that his usually alert teammate, center fielder Bill Virdon, was just as unmindful. Instead of chasing the ball, which was now bouncing toward the ivy-covered wall, Virdon began trotting in alongside Skinner.

Meanwhile, Thomson and Neeman were scampering around the bases. Pittsburgh shortstop Dick Groat was the only Pirate involved in the play who had his head screwed on right. He dashed into left field and yelled at his two oblivious outfielders, "Get the ball! Get the damn ball!"

On the base paths, Neeman couldn't understand why he was still running. When he last looked, he had hit what he thought was just an RBI single. "When I got to second base, I was amazed to see the third base coach waving me on," Neeman recalled. "And when I got near third, he was waving me on home. I had to look around to see if he was waving at somebody else. Nobody ever waved me home before."

Skinner and Virdon, now fully awake, had turned and chased after the ball. But it was Groat who finally tracked it down. Given Neeman's speed—or rather, lack of it—the Pirates still had a chance to throw him out at the plate. But then fate decided to play a cruel joke on them.

"The bleacher fans had thrown all their beer cups and trash down onto the warning track," Skinner recalled. "When we got there, we couldn't find the ball. We finally found it—stuck in a cup! So Dick picked it up and threw it with the ball still inside. But it was too late. Neeman made it all the way around, even though he was the slowest runner in the league."

Talk about slow, how about the minds of Skinner and Virdon? Because of their daze, Neeman's single turned into a three-run homer to win the game 5–2.

Mike Moore

Pitcher

Steve Yeager

Catcher

Seattle, A.L. • April 18, 1986

The Seattle Mariners battery of pitcher Mike Moore and catcher Steve Yeager were as alert as Rip Van Winkle on Sominex.

Incredibly, their inattention allowed a runner to score from second base on a walk!

Pitching in the Kingdome against the Oakland Athletics, Moore got into trouble in the third inning when, with José Canseco on first, Alfredo Griffin doubled. After getting the next two outs on comebackers to the mound, Moore walked Bruce Botche to load the bases. Then the hurler walked the next batter, Dwayne Murphy, to force in the first run of the game.

And that's when Moore and Yeager got burned—scalded, really—by Griffin.

Moore was so angry with himself over the back-to-back walks that when Yeager threw the ball back to him, the irked pitcher bounced it off the artificial turf in disgust. Yeager was also ticked off and turned his back to the pitcher and walked away from the plate.

Meanwhile, Griffin trotted to third on the walk, and, seeing that Moore and Yeager were both mentally off in another world, made a daring dash for home.

When Moore snapped out of his funk and saw Griffin, the hurler panicked. He fired a wild throw that sailed to the backstop, allowing Griffin to score the second run of the inning. The two other A's runners moved to second and third. Moore was so rattled that on the next pitch he gave up a two-run single to Dave Kingman. Those were the only runs Oakland got, but they were enough to beat the Mariners 4–1.

"It was the most bizarre inning I've ever seen," said Seattle manager Chuck Cottier. "I've never seen anything like that before, and I hope I never see it again."

After the game Griffin said, "Neither one of them was paying attention to me. If that happens, I'll try to score."

Moore and Yeager took the blame, as well they should have.

"At first, I didn't hear anybody say anything," Moore told reporters in the clubhouse. "Then I saw Griffin, in plenty of time. When I started to throw, I thought it was Yeager standing at the plate. But it was the umpire. It was too late to hold the ball, and I threw it away."

Yeager, sitting forlornly in front of his locker, admitted, "Griffin surprised both of us. We had just walked a run in and I was aggravated. I turned around and put my back to the play, which apparently I shouldn't have done. I turned around and the ump was kind of standing there. It was just a wide throw. It was just a freak thing."

Cottier described it best: "It's a heads-up play by Griffin, but a heads-down play by us."

BUBBLE GUM BOZOS

◆

Somewhere in those stacks of baseball cards there's a card to suit every taste—bad taste, that is. The bubbleheaded ways some players pose belong in a rogues' gallery instead of a bubble gum card collection. On some cards you have to look real close to find the X-rated message scrawled on a bat or the fly left open on a player's pants. On other cards, a bat or a hand appears to be missing. Then there are those cards in which the text or the cartoon on the back is simply outrageous. For "The Most Unprofessional Baseball Cards," The Baseball Hall of SHAME inducts the following:

Taking the Bat Right Out of His Hands

Gino Cimoli
Topps #286 1958

Snooze Play

Cal McLish
Topps #157 1961

Is That a Baseball Bat,
or Are You Just Glad to See Me?

Jim O'Toole
Topps #70 1963

Clean Up (Your Act) Hitter

 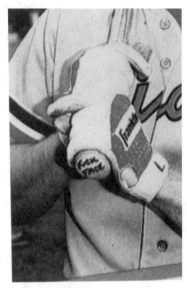

Bill Ripken • Fleer #616 1989

Board with the Game

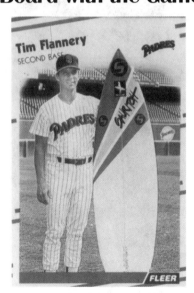

**Tim Flannery
Fleer #582 1988**

An Age-Old Problem

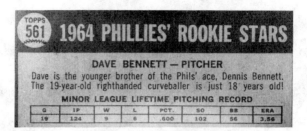

Dave Bennett
Topps #561 1964

Give Him a Hand!

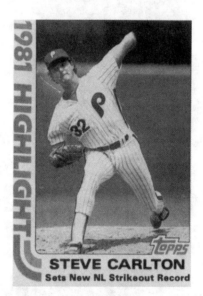

Steve Carlton
Topps #1 1982

Not Enough Zip on It

Norm Cash
Topps #611 1970

Corny Flakes

◆

Flakes defy convention, and often their manager. Because of their antics on the field, their skipper gets gray hair, assuming he hasn't pulled it out already. Flakes play baseball as though their sole purpose on this planet is to drive their manager stark-raving mad. And more often than not they succeed. For "The Daffiest Characters of the Game," The Baseball Hall of SHAME inducts the following:

Frenchy Bordagaray

**Outfielder-Third Baseman • Chicago-New York, A.L.;
Brooklyn-St. Louis-Cincinnati, N.L. • 1934–45**

Frenchy Bordagaray played with such childlike flightiness that his managers wanted to strangle him, but they chose not to because his antics were so hilarious.

Take, for instance, the time in left field when Frenchy ran after a high fly ball, lost his cap, stopped, went back, picked the hat up, put it on, and still made the catch.

Whenever Bordagaray screwed up royally on the field, he uttered one of his wacky, patented lines—he called them Frenchyisms—that always seemed to save his skin.

Frenchy took special delight in infuriating his managers, none more so than Casey Stengel, pilot of the Dodgers during Bordagaray's two-year tour of duty in Brooklyn in 1935–36. "I'd really get Stengel mad," recalled Frenchy with a hearty laugh. "I used to drive him crazy."

In those days, Stengel was managing a second division club and also coaching third base. "One day in 1935 we were playing the Giants in the Polo Grounds," Frenchy recalled. "You know what it was like. You could lose all your other games, but beat the Giants and you still had a good season. Well, I was on second base in the ninth inning of a 1–1 game with two out.

[Teammate] Jimmy Jordan hit a line-drive single to Giants left fielder Jo-Jo Moore. He had an arm like a gun. The ball was in his glove before I even reached third base, but Stengel waved me in."

Bordagaray headed for the plate, but long before he got there, Giants catcher Gus Mancuso was holding the ball and waiting for him. So Frenchy simply stopped dead about 15 feet from home and let Mancuso walk up the line and tag him out.

Stengel rushed from the coaching box and hollered at Frenchy, "That'll cost you 25 dollars for not sliding!"

A red-necked Bordagaray shouted back, "You ought to fine yourself for lousy coaching!"

"Now the fine is 50 bucks!" Stengel retorted with a roar.

"Okay," said Frenchy with a devilish glare. "From now on I'll slide every chance I get." And he stuck to his word.

A few days later Bordagaray belted his only home run of the season. As he headed toward first base, Frenchy realized this was the moment he had been waiting for. "I was still thinking about that fine," he recalled, "so when I saw the ball go over the fence, I said to myself, 'I'll show that son of a gun.'

"I slid into first base. Then I slid into second with a beautiful hook slide, and did the same at third. By now Stengel was out of the coaching box and chasing me toward home. I hit home plate with a terrific headfirst, swan-dive slide. When I looked up, Stengel was standing over me, yelling, 'That'll cost you another 50 bucks for showing me up!' "

Bordagaray cemented his reputation as a flake when he arrived at training camp the next year wearing a big black mustache, the first hairy lip in the majors since Boston Braves catcher John Henry wore one in 1918.

Frenchy sported the mustache because of his off-season job as a part-time Hollywood actor. "The crowds loved it, so I experimented with a goatee too," he said. "But then Casey suggested that I shave it all off. He said, 'I know Brooklyn fans and they are reasonable people, but they do not wish to laugh all the time.'

"I still wanted to keep the mustache, so Casey *ordered* me to shave it off. When I demanded to know why, he said, 'If there's gonna be a clown on this team, it's gonna be me.' "

With Frenchy on the team, Stengel should have known how utterly silly his statement sounded. Bordagaray played as though he had been drafted by Barnum & Bailey. What made him such an endearing flake was his reaction to his screw-ups. At moments when it was prudent to apologize, he would utter a patented Frenchyism, sending his manager into alternating fits of laughter and rage.

For example, there was the game in Cincinnati in 1936 when Bordagaray lost a fly ball—in the *shade*. It was a spring day with bright sunshine and a lot of swift-moving clouds in the sky. George (Moose) Earnshaw was pitching a whale of a game for the Dodgers and led 2–0 with one out in the ninth inning. When a high fly was hit to Frenchy in right field, he settled under it. But just as he flipped down his sunglasses, a cloud blotted out the sun and Bordagaray lost the ball. The batter ended up on third. The next hitter popped up, but an RBI double put the tying run on second base. The Reds' Ival Goodman then whacked a shot deep to right center. This time, Frenchy made a spectacular one-handed catch against the fence to save the game.

In the clubhouse both Earnshaw and Stengel confronted Bordagaray over losing the ball in the shade. The situation seemed to call for a Frenchyism. Turning to Earnshaw, Frenchy said, "Well, George, we sure decoyed them that time. You got Goodman to hit the big one to me in the clutch."

Stengel leaped forward and clamped a headlock on Frenchy. "I'll hold him," Casey told Earnshaw, "and you bite him in the leg." Bordagaray broke free and fled from the clubhouse, just as he had to do the following day in Cincy.

While warming up before the game, Bordagaray let loose with a wild throw that struck Stengel in the ear and knocked him out cold. The players carried Casey to the dugout and revived him. When Stengel came to and learned who had hit him, he snarled, "That guy is gonna go to Podunk tomorrow!" Casey cooled down after the game, which the Dodgers won.

At the clubhouse meeting the next day, Stengel went over the opposition's lineup and then asked if his players had anything to say. Frenchy piped up,

"I hit you in the head yesterday with the ball and we won the game, so that means it's good luck. Let me hit you in the head again and maybe we can win this game, too."

Germany Schaefer

Infielder • Detroit-Washington-New York-Cleveland, A.L.; Chicago, N.L. • 1901–18

Herman "Germany" Schaefer didn't belong on the baseball diamond. He belonged on the vaudeville stage.

He was a clown, a troubadour, an exhibitionist.

The utility infielder was a fun-loving buffoon who tried the patience of his

 UPI/Bettmann Newsphotos

managers because he played with more theatrics than skill. While teammates such as Ty Cobb thrilled fans, Schaefer amused them. He played the game for laughs, often at the expense of his opponents. Usually, his antics would tick off the other team and, in fact, fire them up just to get even.

As a result, Schaefer looked like a doughboy in the trenches because he was always hitting the dirt dodging retaliatory beanballs. He irked Philadelphia Athletics pitcher Rube Waddell to no end in a 1907 game. When Germany belted his first and only home run of the season off Waddell, Schaefer carried his bat with him as he ambled around the bases. About every five paces, he stopped and lifted the bat to his right shoulder as though it were a rifle, and pretended to "shoot" the angry pitcher. Rube wasn't pretending when the next time up he aimed a fastball at Schaefer's head.

Germany's greatest "performance" occurred in 1906 at Chicago's South End Park where the Chicago White Sox were leading the Detroit Tigers 2–1 in the top of the ninth inning. With Detroit runner Charley O'Leary on first, Schaefer was sent up as a pinch hitter. Germany cherished moments like this. Chicago was his hometown, the one place where he wanted to show off.

Since this was in the days before public address systems, umpire Bill Evans blurted out that a pinch hitter had entered the game. That wasn't enough of an introduction for Schaefer. Facing the crowd, he held up his hand for silence, bowed grandly, and then shouted, "Ladies and gentlemen, permit me to introduce myself. I am Germany Schaefer, the world's champion batsman who will now give you a demonstration of his great batting skill."

The stadium erupted in a chorus of boos, hoots, and raspberries. Astute fans knew Germany, who was batting only .238 and hadn't hit a home run all year, was hardly a threat at the plate. "Go back to the bench, you clown!" shouted one Chicago fan. "[White Sox pitcher] Doc White will make a monkey out of you!"

But the crowd was stilled when Schaefer, right on cue, belted the ball over the left-field fence for a two-run homer. Seizing the moment, Germany slid headfirst into first base, picked himself up, and yelled to the stunned fans, "Schaefer leads at the quarter!" Then he sprinted to second base, stopping long enough to announce, "At the half, it's Schaefer by a head!" At third base he bellowed, "Now Schaefer leads by a mile!" Next, he slid majestically into home, where he brushed off his pants, doffed his cap, and proclaimed to the stands, "This, ladies and gentlemen, concludes my afternoon performance."

Germany wasn't afraid to stick it to umpires, too. Once, on a rainy day in Detroit, umpire Tim Hurst refused to call the game. So Schaefer came to the plate wearing a raincoat and boots while carrying an umbrella in one hand and a bat in the other. Hurst gave Germany the old heave-ho. After that, whenever Schaefer was batting and Hurst was umpiring, the vengeful arbiter called any pitch that was even remotely close to the plate a strike.

But that didn't deter Germany. During another game that Hurst was umpiring, Schaefer strode to the plate with a big black false mustache stuck over his lip.

"You're out of the game!" thundered Hurst.

"What for?" argued Germany. "I didn't do anything."

"I don't know what for," replied an exasperated Hurst, "except that you're out of the game!"

Four Ways Dizzy Dean Drove His Manager Crazy

1. In 1937 the brash St. Louis Cardinals hurler bet a teammate he could strike out Boston Braves outfielder Vince DiMaggio every time he faced him that day. DiMaggio fanned his first three times up, but on his fourth at-bat he lifted a pop fly over the head of catcher Brusie Ogrodowski. "Drop it or I'm ruined!" yelled Dean. The catcher let it drop. Then Dizzy burned over the next pitch for strike three.

2. In 1936 Dizzy told Ogrodowski that catchers' signs were a lot of bunk. "I can pitch just as good without them, and I'll prove it." The next day, he went up to Boston Braves manager Bill McKechnie and said, "Catchers get too much credit, so today I'm going to pitch your guys nothing but fastballs. There ain't gonna be no signs." Dizzy then shut out the Braves on four hits.

3. In 1935 Dean promised a hospital ward of crippled kids that he would strike out New York Giants player-manager Bill Terry with the bases loaded. The next day, with the Cardinals clinging to a one-run lead late in the game, the Giants had runners on first and second and two out. Hughie Critz was the next batter, but even though Critz was hitting only .187, Dizzy walked him on purpose—just to get to Terry. Dean then fulfilled his promise to the kids.

4. Just before the start of the second game of the 1934 World Series, when the Cardinals and the Detroit Tigers were supposed to have on their game faces, Dizzy climbed up on a bandstand, picked up a tuba, and played for the fans.

Arlie Latham

Third Baseman • St. Louis, A.L.; Cincinnati, N.L. • 1883–95

No player could frazzle the brain trust of his own team the way Arlie Latham could.

Arlie took it as a personal challenge to see how fast he could make the

OLD JUDGE CIGARETTES Goodwin & Co. New York.

COPYRIGHTED 1888 BY GOODWIN & CO. N.Y.

BROWNS

National Baseball Library

blood boil in St. Louis Browns manager Charlie Comiskey and owner Chris Von der Ahe.

Although he was a remarkable base stealer (109 swipes in 1889) and a decent hitter (.269 lifetime average), the third sacker was less than stellar as a fielder. In fact, his head seemed to be everywhere but in the game.

Rather than dive after hard-hit grounders, or at least block them, Latham acted as though these sizzling smashes had startled him out of a daydream. He'd raise his leg, let out a yelp, and watch the ball zip past him into left field for a base hit. He did this so often that whenever any other third baseman shied away from a hot shot, it was known as "doing an Arlie Latham."

Needless to say, Arlie's play at third base infuriated both Comiskey and Von der Ahe, especially during an 1897 game against Cincinnati. The Reds' Long John Reilly socked a low screaming liner to third, which a startled Arlie deftly avoided with his famous jig. Comiskey, who played first base as well as managed, swore a blue streak. From across the field he shouted, "Wake up, Latham! What are you dreaming about over there?" Arlie just shrugged his shoulders.

A few innings later Reilly stroked another whistling drive down the third base line. Again Latham did an "Arlie Latham" as the ball bounded into left for a double. Comiskey was beside himself with rage and stormed at Latham, "Asleep again, weren't you?"

Arlie didn't say a word. Moments later the diamond was rocked by a loud explosion at third base. Latham turned a couple of somersaults and then crumpled to the ground. Comiskey thought that Arlie had been shot and killed. Just when concern spread across the manager's face, Latham bolted to his feet and announced, "I think I'm awake now." Arlie had placed a lighted firecracker under the bag. For that caper he was fined $50.

But that didn't stop his mind from wandering. Whenever the game got boring, he'd turn from his position on third and strike up a long-distance conversation with the fans. In one game he shouted, "Ladies and gentlemen, please don't go yet. Do you see that church steeple over there? As soon as this game is over, I am personally going to dive off that steeple into a quart of milk." But he didn't stick by his word.

Time and again Latham was fined for paying more attention to the fans in the stands than the action on the field. He was once fined for singing and telling jokes to the crowd while playing third.

Latham, the team leader in fines, loved to aggravate Von der Ahe, who would rant and rave at the Browns whenever they lost a game. One day Arlie locked him out of the clubhouse. Von der Ahe beat on the door and shouted, "This is Chris! This is Chris! Let me in!" Arlie filled a bucket of water, opened the door, and doused his boss. For that splash Latham was fined $50.

After a particularly tough loss, one of the players had torn up the Browns clubhouse. The next day Von der Ahe held a team meeting and demanded to know the name of the culprit. No one came forward. "I'll give 100 dollars to find out who did it," the owner said. Latham's eyes popped open and so did his mouth. "I know who did it," he announced.

"Who?" asked the owner.

"Give me the 100 dollars first," said Arlie. Once the crisp greenbacks were in his grip, Latham said, "I did it."

Von der Ahe let out a howl and bellowed, "For that, I'm fining you 50 dollars!" Then he stomped out of the clubhouse, smug in knowing that no one could put anything over on him. Meanwhile, Arlie walked away with a $50 profit.

During the championship years of the Browns in the mid-1880s, it was customary for the players to parade in single file from the railroad station to their hotel. Von der Ahe, who had a huge bulbous nose and wore a trademark derby hat, always led the parade. Invariably, the crowd of onlookers would break into laughter, much to the owner's bewilderment. Had he bothered to turn around during the march, he would have noticed that Arlie was imitating him by wearing a big red clown nose and a beat-up derby hat.

Lefty Gomez

Pitcher • New York-Washington, A.L. • 1930–43

For New York Yankees manager Joe McCarthy, Lefty Gomez was a pitching joy—and a headache.

The zany hurler helped drive the Yankees to distraction . . . and to six pennants. He capped a Hall of Fame career by chalking up a 26–5 record in 1934 and a 6–0 mark in World Series play. But for all his accomplishments, Gomez is best remembered for his wacky wit and crazy antics on the mound.

They called him "Goofy" for a reason—because he was.

If there was any doubt, it was dispelled in 1938. At the tail end of the season, second baseman Tony Lazzeri enjoyed plenty of good press about his baseball smarts. So Gomez decided to put Lazzeri's reputation to the supreme test in a game against the Detroit Tigers.

Lefty had a comfortable lead in the sixth inning when the Tigers put runners on first and second with nobody out and Hank Greenberg at bat. Greenberg hit a double-play ball back to the mound. Shortstop Frankie Crosetti covered second waiting for Gomez's throw. But Lefty threw it to Lazzeri, who was standing off to the side 20 feet away, and the startled infielder caught the ball in self-defense. All the runners were safe.

Lazzeri charged the mound and sputtered, "Why in the hell did you throw the ball to me?"

"Tony, all I have read in the papers lately is about how smart you are," replied Gomez. "I just wanted to see what you'd do with the ball when you didn't expect it."

A fuming mad Joe McCarthy stalked to the mound and demanded to know why Lefty had pulled such a lamebrained play. "There are too many Italians on this team," Gomez explained with a straight face. "I saw Crosetti and Lazzeri and got confused."

Pointing to center field, McCarthy snapped back, "It's lucky you didn't see DiMaggio."

McCarthy fell off the bench more than once because Gomez stuck his nose in a play that should have been left to the infielders. In a 1940 game against the Tigers, the Yankees caught Barney McCosky in a rundown. Just as Crosetti was about to make the tag, Gomez dashed over and plunged into the action. He triggered a traffic jam and angry shouts from his teammates. Finally, second baseman Joe Gordon tagged out McCosky and then turned on Gomez.

"What the hell were you doing in this?" Gordon snarled. "Why don't you stay on the mound where you belong?"

Whined Lefty, "Why can't I get in on a smart play every once in a while?"

McCarthy gnashed his teeth over Lefty's chronic lapses of concentration.

The sight of an airplane overhead was an irresistible attraction to Gomez. Whenever he saw a plane during a game, he stopped and gawked like a rube. One day Lazzeri strolled to the mound and upbraided him for failing to keep his head in the game.

"Listen, Tony," said Lefty. "You take care of second base and the spaghetti. I'll take care of the pitching and the airplanes."

During the 1936 World Series, Gomez stopped pitching to watch an airplane fly overhead, for which McCarthy came out and chastised him. "If you don't stop looking at airplanes, one of those Giants will rap the ball out of the lot," the manager declared.

"Joe," said Gomez, "if ever one of these guys hits a homer while I'm still holding the ball, then you better take me out, because this racket's getting too tough for me."

In any mound conversation, Lefty always had the last word, which left Marse Joe and his businesslike catcher Bill Dickey muttering to themselves.

In 1936 Gomez gave up one of the longest homers ever hit at Yankee Stadium to Boston Red Sox slugger Jimmie Foxx. This prompted a trip to the mound for McCarthy, who asked his pitcher what he threw Foxx. "I made a great pitch to him—for the first 60 feet," said Lefty. "I fooled him until it got up to him."

In another game Foxx came to bat against Gomez with the bases loaded and no outs. Dickey, who was catching, went through all the signs, but Lefty shook off every pitch.

Finally, Dickey came out and, in a frustrated voice, asked, "Well, what do you want to throw?"

"Nothing," Gomez replied with a shrug. "I'm hoping maybe Foxx will get angry and go sit down."

After watching Dickey catch Lefty for years, people just assumed there was nothing Goofy could do that would surprise Dickey. They were wrong.

One day when the bases were full Lefty beckoned Dickey to the mound. "What's on your mind?" asked the catcher, thinking that Lefty wanted to discuss how to pitch to the next batter.

"Do you have any extra bird dogs back home in Arkansas?" Lefty asked nonchalantly.

Dickey gasped. "Why ask a question like that at a time like this?"

Lefty shrugged and said, "A friend of mine knows you hunt and asked me to find out from you if I ever thought of it. Well, I just thought of it."

No one knew what ridiculous line Gomez would utter during a mound conversation. Once, late in his career, when the flame had flickered from Lefty's fireball, coach Art Fletcher came out to the mound as an emissary from the manager and reported, "McCarthy said to throw harder."

"Throw harder?" asked a shocked Gomez. "I'm throwing twice as hard as I ever did—it's just not as fast."

If it wasn't Lefty's flakiness on the mound, it was his ineptness in the batter's box and on the base paths that drove McCarthy nuts. One day Gomez—who had a .150 lifetime average—hit a double, to the surprise of everyone in the ball park. But moments later he was picked off.

When Gomez returned to the dugout, McCarthy asked angrily, "What happened at second base?"

"How the hell would I know?" replied Lefty. "I've never been there before."

A few years later Gomez socked another double, and the opposing hurler was so upset that he threw a wild pitch, allowing Lefty to reach third. "Hey, Art," Gomez whispered to third base coach Art Fletcher. "I think I can steal home."

Fletcher retorted, "It took you 13 years to get here. What are you trying to do, louse it up?"

If Gomez wasn't driving his manager, coaches, or teammates daffy, he was bedeviling the umpires.

In a 1938 game in Cleveland, the Yankees were losing 5–2 to Indians strikeout king Bob Feller. Late in the game the clouds rolled in and darkened the field, which had no lights back then. New York wanted the umpires to call the game but they refused. So when Gomez went up to bat, he lit a match and held it in front of his face.

Umpire Bill Summers was not amused. "Are you trying to show me up?"

"Certainly not," replied Lefty.

"Well, then, what's the matter with you? Feller's ready to pitch. Can't you see him out there?"

"Sure, I can see him, all right. I just want to make darn sure he can see me."

Another time, shortly before the game, Gomez put on a pair of dark glasses, held a tin cup in his hand, and used a fungo bat as a walking cane. He went out on the field, tapping the ground with his "cane." Then he walked over to umpire John Quinn and said, "Hey, John. Which way is it to the umpires' school?"

Lefty was first tagged with the nickname "Goofy" for a comment he made to New York sportswriter Buck O'Neill. Recalled Gomez, "We were on a road trip and a bunch of us on the train were talking about Einstein and inventors. Buck asked me if I had ever invented anything. I told him, 'Sure, I invented the revolving goldfish bowl.' And he asked, 'What's that?' So I told him, 'In this bowl, the fish doesn't have to keep swimming around in circles all day. He stays in one spot and lets the bowl move. That way, he conserves his energy and lives longer.' The next day he called me 'Goofy' in print. The name stuck ever since."

BOOING THE BOO BIRDS

◆

Fans come to the ball park to watch a game and engage in one of America's favorite pastimes—booing. At the blind umpire, the gopherball pitcher, the slumping slugger. However, sometimes the real boos shouldn't be directed at the playing field, but right up in the stands where fans have displayed some of the rudest, raunchiest, rowdiest behavior this side of a frat party. For "The Wackiest Behavior of Fans," The Baseball Hall of SHAME inducts the following:

Mary "The Horse Lady" Ott

Sportman's Park • 1926–55

With a raucous, scornful, loud hee-hawing laugh, Mary "The Horse Lady" Ott tormented umpires and opposing players at Sportsman's Park in St. Louis for nearly 30 years.

Nicknamed for her shrill, sarcastic whinny, Mary sat behind the home-team dugout at both Cardinals and Browns games. From her box seat, the squat, 180-pound Horse Lady had the lung power to make afternoons miserable for players by jangling their nerves and rattling their concentration.

"I like scientific rooting," she once told a reporter, "something that helps the home boys win and makes the other guys sore. I figure if I really work on them, I can knock a lot of them pitchers out of the box in three innings."

Mary first attracted attention in 1926 when she harassed plate umpire Bill Klem with her insulting braying. The veteran arbiter threatened to have her bodily removed from the park, but she just laughed at him.

"There was never anybody like Mary," recalled Bob Burns, retired reporter for the *St. Louis Globe-Democrat,* who saw—and, more accurately, heard—her at hundreds of games. "She had a voice that you can't describe. Everybody in the stadium could hear her hee-hawing.

"She didn't have specific cheers, or words or yells. She just had this awful screeching laugh. She had a whole repertoire of them. If an opposing player struck out or made an error, she gave a sarcastic, insulting, braying laugh that carried like nothing I've ever heard before."

The Horse Lady drove Philadelphia Athletics Hall of Famer Al Simmons crazy. One time when he struck out, Mary cut loose with one of her special whinnies. Simmons just smiled. When he struck out a second time, Mary really unloaded on him. This time he stomped back to the dugout. The third time up, Mary bellowed her horse laugh while he was in the batter's box. "You could see Al shaking from all the way up in the press box," Burns recalled. "He struck out again and this time he blew up. He thought about going into the stands after her, but some teammates pulled him back. [Manager] Connie Mack had to take him out of the game because he was so shook up."

In the late 1930s Mary loved to harass Philadelphia Phillies outfielder Morrie Arnovich. During a doubleheader she hounded him with her ridiculing laugh. Late in the nightcap she blasted Arnovich just as he was getting ready to swing. "He must have jumped five feet out of the box," recalled Burns. "Then he got into a big argument with the umpire. Morrie waved his bat and pointed over at Mary's box, wanting the umpire to shut her up. The umpire refused. Morrie was so frustrated that he started pounding the ground with his bat.

"Mary knew what she was doing. She really picked her targets. For some reason she liked to go after catchers like Shanty Hogan [Braves and Giants, 1925–35]. Hogan tried to get back at her by imitating her laugh. But he couldn't come close to equaling it."

The Horse Lady wasn't content to torment opposing players on the field. She liked to ambush them after the game at the clubhouse door. Mary let them have it with her sarcastic laugh as they left the stadium.

"They'd run out of the clubhouse and duck into a cab to escape her," said Burns. "She really disturbed some of the players that way. Some would even try to sneak out other exits or find some other way to get back to the hotel before she spotted them."

Just who was the Horse Lady?

"Nobody ever knew exactly who she was or where she came from," said Burns. "There was one story that she was really the madam of one of the city's better houses of ill repute. Another story said that she was the widow of a wealthy plumber. She always loved baseball, but when her husband was alive, he wouldn't let her go to the games. So when he died, she used his money to buy season tickets every year."

Detroit Tigers Fans

Briggs Stadium • 1943

For four hellacious months, Detroit Tigers fans did more to silence the bat of their team's top slugger than any of the league's best pitchers.

In a frightening case of mob psychology, the Briggs Stadium crowd rode Tigers star Rudy York to the verge of a nervous breakdown. Not until sportswriters appealed to the fans for compassion did the booing stop. And when it did, York responded by going on a near-record batting rampage.

York, a powerfully built All-Star first baseman, had been a crowd favorite in Detroit, having led the team to the 1940 World Series with 33 homers and 134 RBIs. He heard nothing but cheers in the confines of Briggs Stadium until the final months of the 1942 season, when he went into a mild batting slump.

When York got off to a bad start in 1943, the hometown faithful began to turn on him. Soon they were blasting him with an incessant flurry of boos, jeers, and catcalls. "Few players in history have ever been ridden harder," reported *The Sporting News* that year. "They boo him from the time his name is announced in the starting lineup until the last man is out. They boo him every time he comes to bat, every time he goes after a batted ball, every time he takes a throw."

The hounding became so unmerciful that York became a wimp at the plate. By July his batting average had plunged to the .200 mark. He was afraid to swing at a pitch for fear he'd trigger a fresh salvo of boos if he missed it. York lost his confidence in the field and wouldn't go after any tough chances because he didn't want to face the fans' wrath if he couldn't make the play. He even became tentative on fielding thrown balls. York was nothing but a shell of the player who the previous year had knocked in 90 runs and set an all-time American League record for assists by a first baseman.

By mid-season York had been booed into a state of nervous collapse. Said *The Sporting News,* "We have seen jittery ballplayers in our time, but none more jittery than York. Not that we blame him; he wouldn't be human had he been able to stand up under the abuse.

"Why should the home crowds boo York? They are supposed to be in his corner, pulling for him. Why should they persecute him?"

Amazingly, it was a question that no one could answer. The scorn that the fans dumped on York went well beyond the typical booing reserved for players in a slump. For some unknown reason, the early-season catcalls snowballed into an avalanche of contempt toward York.

Finally, at the end of July, the Detroit sportswriters came to his rescue. They wrote columns condemning the public persecution of Rudy York and asked for understanding. Where was the sporting spirit of which the United States was so proud? Why deride York? Who, among his booers, had he ever offended? Would one of them have the moral and physical courage to tell him face to face what is said from the safety and security of the stands? How could thousands pick on one man who had not harmed one of them? What sort of hoodlums were attending ball games in Detroit?

Incredibly, the day after the columns appeared, the booing of Rudy York quieted down. Within a few days it had died completely. Jeers gave way to cheers. Buoyed by the new support of the fans, York began swinging with his old carefree abandon. He again took chances on the field.

Up until then, through the first four months of the season, he had hit only 13 home runs and driven in 40 runs. But now, with his self-esteem restored, York went wild at the plate. In the month of August alone, he batted at a sizzling .330 clip, knocked in 42 runs, and walloped an amazing 17 homers—one shy of the major league record for one month. By season's end he topped the league in homers with 34 and RBIs with 118 and broke the league record in assists (which he had set the year before).

Wrote Detroit sportswriter H. G. Salsinger: "We wonder what his 1943 record would have been had he heard the cheers, instead of the jeers of Briggs Stadium customers, from the very start of the season."

Willie Harris

Comiskey Park • Sept. 7, 1960

Willie Harris tried to do what many uncouth fans have had the urge to do—punch a player in the mouth for booting a ball and blowing the game.

Ticked off because he was about to lose a wager, Harris interrupted a game and, before being hustled off to the pokey, took a swing at a player who had screwed up.

It happened during a late-season game in Comiskey Park between the third-place Chicago White Sox and the second-place New York Yankees. As the game began, Harris turned to a friend and made a bet with him that the Sox would win. For a while it looked like Willie was going to collect.

The Sox held a 4–1 lead going into the top of the eighth inning. But then the Yankees launched a rally and had Roger Maris on second and Mickey Mantle on first with one out.

Bill Skowron then hit what appeared to be a made-to-order inning-ending double-play grounder to second baseman Sammy Esposito, who was filling in for an ill Nellie Fox. Unfortunately for Esposito, the White Sox, and Harris, Sammy bobbled the ball and everyone was safe. Instead of the side being retired, New York had the bases loaded. Two hits later the Yankees grabbed a 5–4 lead.

Enraged that he was about to lose some dough because of Esposito's blunder, Willie leaped out of his box seat and raced to the infield, where he confronted Sammy. The hotheaded 41-year-old fan berated Esposito and then took a swing. Sammy ducked and retaliated with a punch of his own. But before either could land a solid blow, players, ushers, and cops grabbed Harris and dragged him away.

After the game, which the Yankees won 6–4, Esposito said, "The guy said something about having money bet on the ball game. I didn't do a thing to him at first. But when he took a swing at me, I swung at him. I didn't hit him. Then the players and ushers came around and broke it up."

As Willie was led away by the police, who booked him on disorderly conduct charges, he mumbled over and over again, "Esposito . . . Esposito . . . Esposito . . ."

New York Yankees Fans

Yankee Stadium • June 18, 1986

New York Yankees fans have never been overly kind to the opposition. But their horrendous treatment of Boston Red Sox rooters makes even Amnesty International wince.

Whenever the Red Sox visit the Bronx, veteran Boston fans know they may be taking their lives in their hands with any show of support for their favorites. God forbid they should ever cheer out loud when their team is winning.

According to members of the Blohards—the Benevolent Loyal Order of Honorable and Ancient Red Sox Diehard Sufferers—Yankee crazies in the upper deck have literally lifted Boston fans out of their seats and passed them around hand over hand to the very edge of the deck. The New Yorkers have swiped Red Sox hats off the heads of rooters and ripped them up, and have swiped Boston pennants and burned them. Sometimes Yankee fans have been known to take bites out of hot dogs as they are passed down the row from vendors to Red Sox fans. In 1989 it became fashionable to dump mustard on Boston backers from the upper deck.

Despite this combat-zone inhospitality, one Boston fan who was either very ignorant or very brave sat in the upper deck of a 1986 game and wore his Red Sox shirt and Red Sox cap and waved his Red Sox pennant. He might as well have been waving a bright red flag in front of a raging bull.

Suzyn Waldman, a reporter for radio station WFAN in New York and a devoted member of the Blohards, was a witness to what happened next.

"First, the Yankee fans took the guy's pennant away from him and threw it down onto the field," she said. "Then they did the same thing with his Red Sox cap."

But that wasn't enough to satisfy their Yankee lust. They surrounded the lone fan, pulled off his Red Sox shirt and ripped the hated team logo to shreds. "Then they pulled his pants off and waved them around as if they had captured a flag in battle. It was really disgusting behavior.

"But you had to give the poor guy credit. He stayed right there cheering for the Red Sox in his undershorts. The Yankee people at least had the decency to leave him that much. They gave him his pants back in time to leave the stadium, but they had stripped him of everything else before the game was over."

Shameful Moments in Fandom

1989—Cincinnati Reds owner Marge Schott tried to catch a pop foul in her front-row box seat, but her young guest snagged it in his glove. Also trying to catch the ball was St. Louis Cardinals catcher Tony Pena. Because Pena likely would have caught the ball, home plate umpire John McSherry called the Cincinnati batter out on fan interference.

1988—During a Chicago White Sox–Boston Red Sox game at Fenway Park, a Red Sox fan jumped from the stands, ran to second base, and mooned the crowd. On one of his buttocks was the word "Jim." On the other was the word "Rice." It was a salute to the Red Sox slugger who had been suspended a day earlier for a run-in with manager Joe Morgan.

1986—When the San Francisco Giants lost a doubleheader to the Los Angeles Dodgers at Candlestick Park, moronic Giants fans took out their frustration by flinging golf balls and even bats at the Dodgers. "The beach at Okinawa was safer," said embarrassed Giants president Al Rosen.

1981—When Oakland Athletics manager Billy Martin stepped out of the dugout during a game with the Minnesota Twins at Metropolitan Stadium, he was barraged with hundreds of marshmallows. They were hurled by Twins fans to remind the former Minnesota manager of his celebrated encounter in 1980 with a marshmallow salesman. Martin had decked the salesman after a barroom bet.

1952—Moments after St. Louis Browns hurler Earl Harrist hit two Boston Red Sox batters in a game at Fenway Park, a one-legged Red Sox fan hobbled onto the field on crutches, went to the mound, and scolded Harrist.

1947—During a game at Wrigley Field, Chicago Cubs fan Paul Ream fell asleep and remained in dreamland even after the game was over. When he awoke later that night, he discovered that all the gates were locked and he couldn't get out. In desperation, he went to a pay phone and called police, who then arranged to free him.

Philadelphia Phillies Fans

The obnoxious behavior of Philadelphia Phillies fans backfired on them when they cost their team a game and snapped the club's hot winning streak.

The Phillies had whipped the New York Giants' 4–0 in the first game of a doubleheader at Shibe Park. But in the nightcap a shameful pop-bottle barrage erupted over a disputed call and forced the umpires to declare a forfeit that went in the record book as a 9–0 victory for the Giants.

The uproar began in the top of the ninth inning with New York ahead 3–2 and a runner on third base. The Giants' Joe Lafata then smacked a sinking line drive to center fielder Richie Ashburn, who appeared to make a shoestring catch.

But to the astonishment of the Phillies and their fans, second base umpire George Barr ruled that Ashburn had trapped the ball. Instead of being out, Lafata ended up on second with a run-scoring double.

"I couldn't believe it," recalled Ashburn. "It was such an obvious catch that everybody in the park saw it except George Barr. It really hurt us because we were on a six-game winning streak and we were still in pennant contention."

The call ignited a firestorm of protest from the Phillies. As the argument raged back and forth on the field, the wrath from irate fans built to a hellish pitch. Suddenly, a soft-drink bottle came flying out of the right-field stands and was answered by a few more from left field.

Within seconds the scattered bottle tossing escalated into an outright artillery bombardment. Players and umpires found themselves caught under a salvo of bottles, vegetables, and cans launched by the ugly crowd of 19,000 soreheads.

Dodging and ducking missilelike bottles, the players frantically weaved their way to the dugouts to escape the barrage. Meanwhile, brave attendants ran onto the field to gather up baskets of trash. The siege lasted for 15 minutes.

Attempts by the public address announcer to calm the crowd were drowned out by booing and catcalls. Even with warnings that the game would be forfeited if the rowdiness continued, the incensed fans refused to stop.

They finally cheered when a well-aimed, overripe tomato splattered on chief umpire Al Barlick and seconds later a bottle grazed the neck of umpire Lee Ballanfant. That did it. Barlick immediately signaled a forfeit and ran for cover with his crew right on his heels.

"That ended our winning streak," said Ashburn. "The only good thing that came out of it was that the state passed a law prohibiting fans from bringing soft-drink and beer bottles into the stadium.

"But it still cost us a game and ended our winning streak. And we had our own Phillies fans to thank for that."

Morganna, the Kissing Bandit

1970–Present

As baseball's most outrageous fan, Morganna, the Kissing Bandit, has been a big bust.

Morganna, who possesses incredible major league stats—an eye-popping 60–24–39—has been arrested 16 times for bouncing out of the stands during games and planting wet smackers on the lips of startled ballplayers.

Through the 1989 season the exotic dancer and stripper has laid lip locks on 24 major leaguers, including New York Yankees star Don Mattingly (see photo). She also got Kansas City Royals superstar George Brett twice. (He got even when he leaped on the stage where she was performing and surprised her with a kiss.)

Morganna, who carries a "hit list" of players to smooch, vows to kiss a player in all 26 ball parks, despite the gritty determination of stadium security forces to stop her.

"I time my kisses so that I never mess up a play," she said. "How many times can a player scratch his balls and spit? There's plenty of time in baseball to run out there and plant a kiss on the cheek and be gone."

The puckering pouncer began her major league career as the Kissing

UPI/Bettmann Newsphotos

Bandit in 1970 at Cincinnati's Riverfront Stadium. "I was with some friends and I kissed Pete Rose on a double-dirty dare," said Morganna. "Who would know that it would snowball into this?"

Among those players Morganna has smooched are:

• Cal Ripken Jr., Baltimore Orioles, 1988—On Fantastic Fans Night, Morganna—wearing pink hot pants and a tight-fitting T-shirt—jumped out of the box seats in right field, bounded all the way to home plate, and planted a kiss on Ripken's cheek. For this heinous crime, she was arrested and tossed in jail, where she spent the night with prostitutes and drug offenders. "They wanted to know what I was in for," she recalled. "I said, 'For kissing Cal Ripken.' They said, 'Where did you kiss him?' I told them I kissed him on the cheek. And they said, 'You got put in jail for *that?*' " The charges were later dropped.

• Fred Lynn, California Angels, 1983—Morganna broke teammate Bobby Grich's heart when she rushed past him in the on-deck circle to get at Lynn. "It feels so good when you're running onto the field and you can hear the fans hooting and hollering and the stadium shaking," she said. "Fred Lynn said he thought it was an earthquake or beach balls when he saw me." After getting bussed, Lynn went down swinging, because, he explained later, "After seeing Morganna coming at me, that baseball looked like a pin head."

• Steve Garvey, Los Angeles Dodgers, 1982—"I must be the only woman he ever ran away from," Morganna said. "We played ring around the umpire. I thought it was because he was a conservative Republican, so I yelled at him, 'I'm a Republican too!' Later I realized he must have thought I was trying to deliver another paternity suit. But I got him. Afterward, Steve sent me an autographed picture that said, 'Morganna, your pucker is prettier than mine.' "

• Nolan Ryan and Dickie Thon, Houston Astros, 1985—"This was one of the few times I announced my intentions in advance," Morganna said. "By the time I got to the Astrodome, there were more cops in the aisles than ushers." But there was too much Morganna for one cop. She leaped onto the field and streaked to the mound. Ryan dropped to one knee, spread his arms, and implored, "Hurry up, Morganna! The cops are right behind you!" After smooching Ryan, Morganna kissed a stunned Dickie Thon at shortstop. As the cops took her away, she shouted, "My first double play of the season!"

Normally, Morganna is charged with trespassing and released on $200 bond, which she forfeits. But in Houston the district attorney got mean about it and booked her on criminal trespassing, which carries a $5,000 fine and/or a year in jail.

Morganna's attorney, Richard "Racehorse" Haynes, announced he would use the gravity defense: "This woman with a 112-pound body and 15-pound chest leaned over the rail to see a foul ball. Gravity took its toll, she fell out on the field, and the rest is history." The case was dismissed.

Morganna said she never wants to go into the slammer again because she wouldn't look good in prison stripes. Added the Kissing Bandit, "Stripes make me look top-heavy."

Joe "Angel Ape" Badame

California Angels Fan • 1980

Joe Badame donned an ape suit and pranced around Anaheim Stadium to stir up team spirit. Instead he stirred up nothing but trouble—for himself, the fans, and the team.

When the 1980 season rolled around, the California Angels were touted as the team to beat because they were the previous year's American League West champions. Pennant fever had already struck Angels fans—especially Badame, a 35-year-old part-time magician and roofer. Swept up in all the excitement, he became a self-proclaimed cheerleader.

First he fashioned a homemade halo out of a coat hanger and aluminum foil. But a halo by itself didn't make much of a statement. "Suddenly, I had this idea to wear a gorilla suit to the game on Opening Day," Badame recalled. "I put it on, fixed the halo on a kind of frame so it hung over my head, and went to the stadium."

Security officers, citing a rule against wearing masks in the stadium, refused to let the synthetic simian through the gate. But after Badame convinced them he was harmless, they relented. It turned out to be a regrettable mistake.

Badame—dubbed the Angel Ape—became a regular at Angels home games, where he roamed the aisles and led cheers. For a while he was tolerated by the fans and club management. But not for long.

Fans began to gripe about him and found his ape suit offensive. It was slightly decrepit and decidedly smelly. Whenever he found a place to sit down, the fans sitting nearby got up and moved. "We couldn't make him stay in his seat, because then those nearby complained about how he smelled," Buzzie Bavasi, the club's executive vice president, told the press.

Then there was the matter of Badame's annoying cheerleading. A souvenir vendor had paid the Angel Ape's admission to games in exchange for the gorilla using the vendor's booster towels during the Ape's monkeyshines. The Ape roamed the stadium waving a towel in the faces of fans, exhorting them to cheer for the team—and, not coincidentally, to buy more towels. But he often blocked their view of the game. Soon the cries of "Down in front!" far outnumbered those of "Go Angels!"

Other fans complained that the Angel Ape terrorized kids. Although he may have thought he was funny, wide-eyed little tykes thought a big, smelly ape running up to them was scary. The kids cringed in terror.

Even so, the Angel Ape might have survived the simmering crowd resentment except for a curious fact: The Angels were losing. In fact, the club was headed downhill faster than a California mudslide. Everyone was searching for a reason.

Angels center fielder Rick Miller was the first to come up with an answer. "It's that damn Angel Ape," he groused. "He's jinxed us."

Echoed teammate Don Baylor, "He wasn't around last year, and ever since he appeared, we haven't won."

The jinx theory spread like wildfire. By June, with the team mired in the cellar, the front office felt compelled to act. It was time for the cheerleading chimp to find a new vine to swing on. The Angel Ape was banned.

When Badame was told his alter ego would no longer be welcome at Anaheim Stadium, he griped, "Why are they blaming me? I'm not on their pitching staff."

Brooklyn Dodgers Fans

Ebbets Field • 1916

Brooklyn Dodgers fans heaped such a torrent of abuse on their own shortstop, Ivy Olson, that he never took the field without first stuffing cotton in his ears!

"I understood them," Olson recalled years later. "They said they hated me, but I knew they loved me."

The Ebbets Field fans sure had a strange way of showing their affection. They loved to taunt Olson, a spike-scarred, swarthy veteran with a barrel chest, bowed legs, and a misguided throwing arm.

In 1916, shortly after Ivy was traded to Brooklyn, the Flatbush faithful began calling him "Ivan the Terrible." That was understandable. His parenthetical legs formed a circle through which grounders skipped into left field. When he did glove a hard smash, his too-strong arm occasionally rocketed the ball into the first base boxes. Once, a wild throw by Ivy hit manager Wilbert Robinson right in the stomach as he sat in the dugout.

Although Ivy racked up the second highest number of errors for a shortstop that season, he was nonetheless a fighter and a fine clutch hitter—traits conveniently overlooked by the fans. So was the fact that he helped bring the pennant to Brooklyn that year.

Instead, they booed him so ferociously that the only way Olson could play was with cotton in his ears.

He began wearing the plugs after coming back from an early-season road trip. Although he had made several errors during the previous home stand, Ivy had played extremely well on the road. "The newspapers in St. Louis, Cincy, and Chicago said what a big help I was to the Dodgers," Olson recalled. "You know, 'Olson Sparks Dodgers,' stuff like that.

"Well, my first day back at Ebbets Field, I'm taking infield practice and the first ball Uncle Robbie [manager Wilbert Robinson] hits to me goes whoosh right through my legs. The fans start riding me. Robbie hits me another. She skips through, too. The fans really get on me. So for the rest of the practice, I let everything go through just to steam 'em up real good.

"Just before the game I get two long pieces of cotton from [trainer] Doc Hart. I come out and stick them in my ears so I won't hear the fans riding me. It works. I don't hear the boos.

"But every time I make a good play, I make a big deal of taking the cotton out of my ears like I'm waiting to hear the applause. So what do they do? They boo me even more!"

From then on the hometown fans gave him nothing but grief.

Once, during a 1916 game at Ebbets Field, Olson hit a two-run triple that put the Dodgers ahead late in the game. As he stood proudly on third, a group of Brooklyn fans in the box seats were giving him hell. "Ivan the Terrible, you stink!" shouted one guy. His buddy yelled, "Olson, you bum! Get outta town!"

Ivy noticed that it was the same group who had been riding him for the last few days. So after the third out he moseyed over to their box. "Gents," he said, "you paid your way in and it's your right to ride me. I admit I skipped a couple of grounders [made a few errors] in this series, so it was only right for you to get on me. But I just hit a triple and you hopped on me again. Why?"

"It's like this," said one of the fans. "We think you're playing just to aggravate us. Two days ago, when you got two hits to win the game, we had bet against the Dodgers. Yesterday we bet on the Dodgers and they lost because of your error. Today, we bet against the Dodgers and you hit a triple. If you win today, we're out five grand. What are you trying to do? Ruin us?"

Fully understanding their motives, Olson said, "At least *you* have a reason to rag me. But the rest of the fans . . ."

HEAVE HO-HO'S

♦

Although umpires don't see all the things they should, they usually hear all the things they shouldn't. Baseball has a rich tradition of umpire baiters who catch hell by casting a steady stream of insults that turn the men in blue a shade of red. What often follows is a heated argument that ends when the arbiter thumbs his antagonist out of the game. For "The Most Inglorious Ejections from a Game," The Baseball Hall of SHAME inducts the following:

Ray "The Deacon" Murray

Catcher • Baltimore, A.L. • April 25, 1954

Not even divine intervention could save Baltimore Orioles catcher Ray Murray from an unscheduled trip to the showers. In fact, he was still down on his knees praying at the plate when an even greater power—the umpire—gave him the thumb.

It was the holiest ejection in baseball history.

Murray was known as the Deacon because he was an evangelist who practiced his "Old Time Religion" among the heathen ball players and pagan umpires. Unlike most of those around him, Ray seldom swore. Instead, he found creative ways to express his displeasure over what he considered the blind injustice of American League umpires.

One of those whose eyesight Murray felt to be most in need of prayer was the no-nonsense arbiter, Ed Hurley. The two got along about as well as a preacher and an infidel. It didn't take a prophet to know they would trigger some hell-fire.

Ray and Hurley clashed in baseball's most pious heave-ho—one spurred by the ump's earlier banishment of Murray.

"I always accused Hurley of carrying the Yankees meal money with him," Ray recalled. "One day, in a game at Yankee Stadium, we had two runners on base. We had a guy at the plate with a 3-and-2 count on him with two out. The next pitch was so high the catcher had to jump up to get it.

"That should have been ball four and loaded the bases, but Hurley, who was working behind the plate, called out, 'Steerrriikkke threeeee!' Lordy, you should have seen the stuff that flew out of our dugout—bats, towels, everything that wasn't nailed down.

"I was still stomping mad when I went out to catch in the bottom half of the inning. The first pitch was a perfect strike, but Hurley called it a ball. I turned around and asked, 'Ed, just how much you got bet on this game?' He threw me out right then and there."

Murray was determined not to let the ejection pass without a little eye-for-an-eye and tooth-for-a-tooth righteousness. He got his chance when the Orioles played a double-header against the Chicago White Sox and Hurley was one of the umpires.

Since he didn't play in the first game, Ray used the time on the bench to repeatedly hurl an insult Hurley's way: "You're an S.O.B.—the Same Old Boy who robbed us before!"

Hurley fumed throughout the first game, but kept his temper in check. However, in the nightcap, with Murray catching and Hurley umpiring behind the plate, it was only a matter of time before the two would clash. They held off until the bottom of the ninth when the Sox, trailing 3–2, had Freddie Marsh on first with no out and Cass Michaels at bat.

"There was a full count on Michaels and Marsh took off on the next pitch, which was right down the middle," Murray recounted. "I mean, there was no question about it. I caught the ball waist high and fired the ball to second base.

"Then I saw all the umps with their arms in the air and Hurley was behind me bellowing, 'Ball four!' I couldn't believe it. I had a few good words that I wanted to say to him, but I knew it wouldn't do any good."

Instead of blowing up, Murray calmly and deliberately took off his mask, removed his chest protector, and carefully spread it over home plate. Then he got down on his knees, stretched his arms wide, looked heavenward, and implored, "Oh Lord! Help this poor S.O.B. I got two good eyes. Give him one of mine!"

Baltimore manager Jimmy Dykes bounded out of the dugout and raced to home plate, hoping to save his catcher from getting the thumb. But Dykes was too late. The enraged umpire pointed to Murray, who was still on his knees, and bawled to Dykes, "Get this guy outta here or it'll cost him a 1,000-dollar fine!"

Dykes jerked to a stop, removed his hat, and held it over his heart. "No sir," Dykes replied piously. "Not while the man is still praying!"

The Mouth that Soared

In 1980, when Don Zimmer managed the Boston Red Sox, he got into many heated arguments, including one with umpire John Shulock.

During the dispute, Zimmer angrily took the chaw out of his mouth and slammed it down into the dirt. Then Shulock threw his chaw down. But Zimmer had to call a truce. When he flung his chaw, his false teeth had gone with it.

Tony Gwynn

Right Fielder • San Diego, N.L. • April 17, 1988

The first and only time Tony Gwynn was ever ejected from a game happened because Tony dared the umpire to throw him out—so the ump did.

Gwynn, one of baseball's calmest and most considerate players, lost his cool during an early-season game in 1988 between the San Diego Padres and the visiting San Francisco Giants.

In the third inning Gwynn took a pitch from Kelly Downs that plate umpire Joe West called a strike. Uncharacteristically, the batting champion began jawing with West. One word led to another and the two engaged in a full-scale brouhaha.

Padres manager Larry Bowa, no stranger to arguments, raced out onto the field to act as a peacemaker. But by now Gwynn was on fire, and literally threw Bowa aside as he continued to chew out the umpire.

Finally, Gwynn snarled at West, "It's not a strike, and if you don't like it, you can throw me out."

"Okay," snapped the ump. "You're out of the game!"

Later, West told reporters, "That's the first time a player has ever told me to throw him out of a game."

In the clubhouse Gwynn said, "Usually when I don't like a call, I back down. But I felt I was at the point where it was put up or shut up. So I decided to put up. I just lost it."

Danny MacFayden

Pitcher • Pittsburgh, N.L. • 1940

Danny MacFayden was ejected from the same game twice. He first got tossed for showing up an umpire over a disputed call. But when his manager tried to intervene, the red-hot MacFayden only made matters worse by showing up the arbiter again, spurring a second thumb.

Danny was on the mound for the Pittsburgh Pirates in a 1940 game against the Philadelphia Phillies. The fiercely competitive bespectacled hurler was pitching his heart out midway through a tight contest when the batter worked the count to 3-and-2.

On the next pitch, MacFayden threw a fastball that he was sure had nicked the outside corner. But plate umpire Bill Klem called, "Ball four!"

The veteran pitcher couldn't believe the call. He charged off the mound and whipped off his glasses on his way to confront Klem. When he reached home plate, the irate MacFayden handed his specs to Klem and shouted at the top of his lungs, "Here, you take 'em! You need 'em more than I do!"

With one imperious gesture, Klem gave Danny the thumb. "You're out of the game!" bellowed the ump. "Now head for the showers!" Pirates manager Frankie Frisch, who'd seen more than his share of thumbs during his playing career, ran onto the field to cop a plea for his hurler. Frisch told Danny to stay put and then tried to mollify the outraged arbiter.

"Bill, please give me a break," begged Frisch. "I'm in a tough spot. I'm really short of pitchers. Danny was only kidding. Fine him tomorrow, but let him stay in the game today. He was just excited. You can't put him out for just taking off his glasses. Look, he's wiping them. That's why he took them off. Please, Bill, have a heart."

The vexed umpire shook his head. "That gag about the glasses didn't bother me," said Klem. "[Giants manager] John McGraw used that one on me 30 years ago. I'm not putting MacFayden out for casting aspersions on my eyesight. But, Frank, it's the way he was showing up an umpire. He was yelling so loud that everybody in the stands could hear him. He yelled to incite the crowd, to cause a commotion, and possibly a riot. That's a flagrant violation."

Before Frisch could say another word in defense of his pitcher, Danny butted in and snarled at Klem, "I didn't yell to incite the crowd. The only reason I talked so loud was I was afraid your ears were as bad as your eyes!"

"You're outta here!" Klem bellowed once more.

Frisch moaned like a wounded bear and waved weakly toward the bullpen for another pitcher.

Frankie Frisch

Manager • St. Louis-Pittsburgh-Chicago, N.L. • 1933–51

Tempestuous Frankie Frisch was famed for his battle royales with umpires, yet he counted among his close friends three of the game's greatest arbiters—Bill Klem, Jocko Conlan, and Beans Reardon.

That didn't stop his friends in blue from giving Frankie the old heave-ho more than any other manager of his day.

Knowing he could never get in the final say with the umps, Frisch gained some satisfaction by finding new ways to exasperate the arbiters. Bill Klem—the king of umpires—proved a real challenge.

To thwart protesting players, Klem would trace a line on the ground with his foot, glower, and say, "If you cross that line, you're out of the game." And if they did, they were.

In 1934 Frisch, then player-manager of the St. Louis Cardinals, got into a brouhaha with Klem, who then drew his line. So Frankie started to circle to Klem's right and go around the end of the line. Klem drew another line. Frisch kept circling until the veteran ump had drawn four lines and completely boxed himself in.

"Now see what you've done," chortled Frankie. "Hey, wise guy, how are you gonna get outta *there?*"

"You're not gonna find out, 'cause you're outta *here!*" bellowed Klem, giving Frisch the heave-ho.

When Frankie was playing for the New York Giants in 1926, he tried a sneaky way to show up Klem at the plate. Whenever Klem called a pitch a strike that Frisch thought was a ball, he stepped out of the batter's box, shook his head, turned to the umpire, and, with arms flailing, said sweetly, "That sure was a dandy, wasn't it? Just caught the corner." Not privy to the conversation, the hometown fans assumed that Frisch was telling Klem off but good and they began to boo the ump.

Klem tried to stop Frankie by decreeing absolute silence in the batter's box under penalty of banishment. Frisch kept testing Klem and flunked each time. The Fordham Flash shelved that particular tactic after he was ejected three times in one season for the same innocuous remark: "We sure could use some rain, Bill."

Frisch's most memorable exit at the thumb of Klem came in 1933 when the ump called a Cardinal out on a bang-bang play. As manager, Frankie blew his top and argued strenuously for several minutes. Suddenly he keeled over backward and lay absolutely still.

Players and coaches rushed from both dugouts, the trainers dashed to Frisch's side, and a doctor was summoned as a huge circle formed around the prostrate skipper. It looked like a heart attack induced by a bum decision.

Klem stood to the side, rightfully suspicious of Frisch's sudden heart attack. Then he waded through the group, stood directly over Frankie, and snarled, "Frisch, dead or alive, you're out of the game!"

Some of Frisch's best theatrics were pulled on Jocko Conlan. Frankie received rave reviews from the fans, but the only notices he got from Jocko were evictions.

In a 1941 game against the Brooklyn Dodgers at Ebbets Field, Frisch, then manager of the Pittsburgh Pirates, was irked because umpires refused to suspend play when it began to rain. With his team trailing by a run in the third inning, he shouted to Conlan, "All my players will get pneumonia, but you haven't got enough guts to call the game."

Jocko retorted, "What's the matter? Haven't you got guts enough to play it?"

At the start of the next inning Frisch headed out of the dugout with a raised umbrella to drive home his point that Jocko should know enough to come in out of the rain.

Conlan gave him a dandy jerk of his thumb and shouted, "Take that umbrella with you!"

Frisch protested, "What's the matter? Can't a guy have a little fun?"

"Have all you want to," said Jocko. "But not at *my* expense."

Even when Frisch was right, his flair for theater got him bounced. In a 1944 game against the Chicago Cubs, the Pirate skipper was coaching third base. Pittsburgh runner Frankie Zak was on first when Jim Russell belted an extra-base hit. As Zak rounded third, Cubs third baseman Eddie Stanky gave him the hip and sent Zak skidding halfway to the dugout.

"Interference! Obstruction! Dammit, I don't know what the hell it is, except it's wrong and my man scores!" Frisch hollered to Jocko, umpiring at third. "You're right," said Conlan. "It's obstruction and he scores."

Meanwhile, Russell was trying for a triple. Just as the runner began his slide into third, Frisch stunned everyone by sliding into the bag himself from the coach's box.

Surveying this bizarre situation, Jocko pointed to Russell and shouted, "You're safe!" Then turning to Frisch, the arbiter said, "And you're out—out of the game!"

As he dusted himself off, Frankie grumbled, "How about that? Here, I make the best slide I've made in 15 years, and I get put out of the game."

Frisch took perverse delight in matching wits with umpire Beans Reardon. Frankie knew that Beans would rather exchange sulfuric insults than pull his rank. So the two engaged in some classic cheek-to-jowl arguments. But every once in a while Reardon would throw Frisch off stride by sending him to an early shower.

Once, in a 1940 game, Reardon called a close play against the Pirates, prompting Frisch to leap from the dugout in protest and unleash a torrent of epithets.

"What did you say?" demanded Beans.

"You've been guessing all afternoon, why don't you guess what I said?" Frankie shot back.

Throwing his thumb up in the air, Reardon thundered, "Guess what this means!"

Beans was the umpire who once *refused* to eject Frankie, even though Frisch wanted to get tossed.

Before a double-header in Brooklyn on a beautiful sunny day in 1935, Frisch was suffering from painful lumbago. He wanted desperately to go to his home in nearby New Rochelle to tend to his rose garden. But as player-manager of the Cardinals, he could hardly take the day off. That would be quitting. However, if he were ejected early in the first game . . . well, that was a different matter.

In his first at-bat he waited until Beans called a strike. Then Frankie went into action. "What?" he howled. "Why, you blind ox! A mile outside and you call it good. Haven't you any conscience?"

Puzzled that he wasn't getting a rise out of Reardon, Frisch launched into another act. He threw his bat to the ground, tossed his hat, and kicked the dust.

"Just a minute, Frankie," Beans said gently. "Just get back in there and swing, because you're planting no roses in New Rochelle today!"

The remark stunned Frisch into silence and he meekly returned to the batter's box and played the double-header. Only weeks later did he learn that teammate Pepper Martin had tipped off Reardon about the scheme to get the day off.

Timely Ejection

Casey Stengel discovered that even talking politely and without profanity could still get him the heave-ho.

During a 1940 game, Stengel, then manager of the Boston Braves, got into a prolonged argument with umpire Bill Klem. The veteran arbiter then pulled out a watch and said, "You have 30 seconds to leave the field."

"Gee, Bill," said Casey. "You're crazy to show that watch in front of this crowd. Its owner may recognize it."

Everyone in the stands recognized Klem's subsequent gesture for ejection.

Granny Hamner

Shortstop • Philadelphia, N.L. • June 21, 1957

Granny Hamner was kicked out of a game after arguing over a play in which he was called *safe!*

In a game against the Milwaukee Braves, the Philadelphia Phillies infielder hit a bouncer to deep short, where Johnny Logan made a hurried throw that pulled Frank Torre off first base. Torre made a desperate swipe at Hamner as he raced by, but Torre missed him.

As he crossed the bag, Hamner yelled, "No! No!" It was his way of saying that he had not been tagged.

But first base umpire Ken Burkhart took exception to Hamner's words. "I'm doing the umpiring here," said the arbiter caustically. Alluding to Hamner's previous run-ins with umps, Burkhart added, "In fact, you've been umpiring long enough."

Hamner shouted back, "Hey, it's a free country. I can say what I want, especially when it's true."

Like spontaneous combustion, the verbal exchange flared into a full-scale dispute as players from both sides wondered why a player would argue over being called safe. Finally, Burkhart warned, "One more word out of you and you're gone."

"One more word," said Hamner sarcastically.

So Burkhart gave him the heave-ho. Incredibly, Granny Hamner was safe and out on the same play.

Bobby Bragan

Manager • Pittsburgh-Milwaukee-Atlanta, N.L.; Cleveland, A.L.
1956–58, 1963–66

As a temperamental manager, Bobby Bragan took great pleasure in embarrassing umpires.

Bobby originated the modified striptease to show his disgust over a decision. He refined the sit-down strike. And he honed his skills at agitating arbiters by offering them a swig of a soft drink.

Bragan's outrageous umpire-baiting capers began in the minor leagues, where he set records for the number of fines and ejections. In five years as a Texas League manager, Bobby was given the thumb an incredible *sixty* times.

The most infamous incident occurred at Oklahoma City, when Bragan refused to leave the field after a particularly animated argument with the umpires. So the fed-up arbiters ordered a policeman to haul Bobby away. Bragan saw the cop coming and took off for center field. The lawman, a 240-pounder not especially built for speed, chased Bobby from center field to left, then back to the infield and around the bases before finally nailing him near the dugout.

UPI/Bettmann Newsphotos

In the Pacific Coast League, Bragan sharpened his act. One day, in a quarrel with future major league umpire Chris Pelekoudas, Bobby pointed to the ump's large nose and said bitingly, "Now that's a perfect reason for you to miss the call. With a nose like that, how can you be expected to see around it?"

The cruel remark cost Bobby $50. A short time later he drew a three-day suspension for his celebrated striptease act in San Diego. Following a brouhaha, Bragan, who managed and caught for the Hollywood Stars, was ejected. So Bobby began shedding his gear and throwing it out onto the field. First came the chest protector, then shin guards, mask, glove, and cap. Retreating to the dugout, he brought his performance to a hot finish by tossing out his uniform top, shoes, undershirt, and a towel.

The subsequent suspension still didn't thwart Bragan's penchant for belittling the men in blue. The following year Bobby got into a heated rhubarb with future major league umpire Emmett Ashford. When Bobby angrily flung his cap against the backstop, Ashford feared another striptease and ordered him from the field. Bragan had other ideas.

To show up the umpires, he stretched out on his back at home plate with one arm supporting his head and his knees crossed nonchalantly. Bragan remained there for a few minutes, sunning himself and thumbing casually through a newspaper which a peeved fan had thrown at him.

On another occasion a fuming Bragan claimed that the umpires were making a farce of the game. So he did them one better—he sent the batboy out to coach third base! Another time, in protest over a call, Bobby dispatched a pinch hitter to the plate, replaced him with another pinch hitter, and continued until he had used nine pinch hitters for the original batter.

As a parting gesture after getting the heave-ho in another game, Bragan departed by pretending to be a blind man fumbling his way across the field. He kept his hands outstretched and walked smack into a light pole. The fans laughed. The umps seethed.

Bobby's most famous umpire-baiting stunt occurred in the majors during a game against the Milwaukee Braves in 1957 when he was managing the Pittsburgh Pirates. When umpire Stan Landes called a Milwaukee runner safe, Bragan held his nose to show the ump what he thought of the decision. So Landes ejected him.

"Just a minute, Stan," shouted Bobby from the dugout. "I want to talk this thing over with you. But you'll have to wait while I get a hot dog and an orange drink."

One of his players, Whammy Douglas, bought a carton of orange drink from a vendor and handed it to Bragan, who didn't wait for the hot dog. Sipping the drink through a straw, Bobby walked onto the field as the County Stadium crowd guffawed. He went up to crew chief Frank Dascoli and offered him a drink. "Have a sip," said the manager. "There's plenty for all of us."

"Scat," said the annoyed arbiter. So Bragan sauntered over to first base umpire Frank Secory and asked him if he'd like a sip. The ump declined, saying, "Why don't you cut out this bush-league stuff." To show he had no ill feelings against Landes—the man who threw him out—Bobby offered the ump a swig, but was refused. Finally, Bragan tried arbiter Bill Baker, who also declined.

But things turned nasty when Dascoli bellowed, "Get out of here or I'll forfeit the game."

"You don't have that much guts," hissed Bobby.

When Secory intervened, Bragan threatened, "I'll throw this drink in your face."

Secory stuck out his jaw and said, "Let's see you try."

But Bobby chose a more discreet course—the one leading to the club-house.

It was the second time he had shown up the umpiring crew. Earlier in the year he had two of his players lug a bucket of water around outside the dugout during a game as a hint to the men in blue that Cincinnati Reds pitcher Raul Sanchez was throwing spitballs.

The orange-drink caper riled National League president Warren Giles so much, he fined Bragan $100 and warned him that a repeat performance would result in an indefinite suspension. "It is not in your nature to take the game seriously," Giles told him in a telegram. "We and others consider it serious business."

Pirates general manager Joe L. Brown considered it so serious that he fired Bragan two days later.

Say What?

In a 1970 game against the Cincinnati Reds, Ron Swoboda of the New York Mets hit what appeared to be a grand-slam home run. His drive hit above the yellow line halfway up the Crosley Field center-field fence. The bottom half of the fence was concrete, the top half plywood. But the umps said the ball hit below the yellow line.

Mets coach Yogi Berra was certain the ball had hit above the line, off the plywood. Berra argued with the umpires, who then threw him out when he uttered this classic Yogism: "Anyone who can't tell the sound of a ball bouncing off concrete or wood is blind."

Jimmy Dykes

Manager • Chicago, A.L. • June 7, 1942

Jimmy Dykes was fined so often for arguing with umpires that he could have set up a separate checking account solely to pay off all the fines.

His wildest transgression cost him two ejections and two fines—and lasted a whole week.

His Chicago White Sox were playing the nightcap of a Sunday double-header in Boston against the Red Sox late in the afternoon. There was a blue law in Boston at the time which said Sunday baseball games had to end by 6:30 P.M.

At 6:20 P.M. the Red Sox came to bat in the bottom of the eighth with the score tied 2–2. The first two batters singled, putting runners at first and third with no out.

It was now 6:22 P.M. Dykes knew that if Chicago could hold off Boston for eight more minutes, the game would be called and the White Sox would at least salvage a tie.

He had to stall. Dykes called time and moseyed out to the mound, where he was met by umpire Ed Rommel. "Are you changing pitchers?" asked the ump.

"I haven't decided yet," said the manager.

"You're stalling," said the ump. "Now make up your mind."

"Okay, I want the righty."

So Rommel raced down toward the bullpen and signaled for relief pitcher Joe Haynes, who slowly ambled in and then intentionally walked the next batter to load the bases. It was 6:25 P.M. Five more minutes to go. Dykes called time, raised his left hand, and walked back to the mound. Seeing Dykes's left hand go up, Rommel again took off for the bullpen, where right-hander Pete Appleton and left-hander Jake Wade were warming up. Rommel grabbed Wade by the arm and hurriedly dragged him to the mound.

"Who's this?" Dykes asked Rommel in mock surprise.

"It's Wade, your lefty," replied the ump.

"I don't want a lefty," said Dykes. "I want Appleton."

"Look, Jim," said the arbiter. "I know everything that's going on in that mind of yours. You're trying to kill time until 6:30. If I have to stop every clock in Boston, we're going to finish this inning!"

Dykes and Rommel then jawed nose to nose until the ump squashed the argument. "We're not wasting another second! You're out of the game! Now get going!"

Dykes was led away protesting as the ump ordered Wade to pitch to the next batter, Lou Finney. On a 2–0 pitch Finney lifted a fly ball to center that scored the winning run. The game was then called as the clock ticked to 6:30.

Dykes filed a formal protest. However, American League president Will Harridge not only denied the protest, but fined the manager $250 for delaying the game.

Burned to a crisp, Dykes vowed revenge. He got it a week later before a game in Washington where the same umpiring crew was working.

Dykes sent his coach Mule Haas up to the plate with the White Sox lineup card and handed it to Rommel. The arbiter looked at it and then said, "Wait a minute, Mule. You've got only eight players listed here. Where's the other one?"

Without batting an eye, Haas said, "Dykes told me to tell you that since you did such a helluva fine job picking his pitcher for him in Boston last Sunday, he wants you to do it again today." Dykes and Haas were immediately ejected. Said Dykes later, "It sure was worth it."

It felt almost as good as the heave-ho he got during a game with the New York Yankees a few years earlier. Dykes felt every close call by umpire Bill Grieve went against the White Sox. Naturally, the fiery manager disputed every one of the calls. In the seventh inning Dykes charged the ump for the fourth time that day, and as the hot skipper ranted and raved, Grieve acted like a thoroughly bored listener.

Finally, in his fit of rage, Dykes yanked off his White Sox cap, threw it away, and pulled a Yankee hat out of his pocket. He jammed it on his head and boldly announced, "This ought to get me a decision!"

It got him one—but not the one he wanted. He received a $50 fine and a three-day suspension.

Getting Hit from the Blind Side

Baltimore Orioles manager Earl Weaver was thrown out of more games than any other skipper in his time.

In a 1972 game he raised hell with the umpires over a seldom-called rule that went against his team. "I know the rules as well as you do," he declared. "I've got a book in the clubhouse to prove it."

"I've got the book with me now," said the umpire. "I'll show you."

"That's no good," snapped Weaver, "because I can't read Braille!" He definitely read the meaning of the ump's thumb.

Shameful Heave-Ho's

1988—Cincinnati Reds infielder Dave Concepcion was ejected from a game for blowing kisses at second base umpire Dave Pallone.

1987—San Francisco Giants manager Roger Craig (shown in photo) was tossed out of a game *after* it was over. Umpire Doug Harvey called a game-ending balk that gave the Philadelphia Phillies a 9–8 victory. Craig had a few choice words for Harvey at the conclusion of the game and got the boot en route to the clubhouse.

1965—Los Angeles Dodgers pitcher Mike Kekich got thrown out of a major league game before he actually played in one. Kekich had joined the Dodger bench jockeys in riding an umpire. Suddenly they all quit yapping at once, except Kekich, whose ensuing cutting remarks brought him the thumb. "That won't happen again," said veteran teammate Wally Moon. "All the kid needs is to get his timing down pat."

1948—Charlie Grimm, manager of the Chicago Cubs, was ejected from a game because he was too friendly with an umpire. After losing an animated argument with one arbiter, Grimm walked over to ump Jocko Conlan and put his arm around Jocko's shoulder. "You're outta here!" roared Conlan. When Grimm asked why, Jocko said, "If you think you're going to show up my buddy by being palsy-walsy with me, you're crazy."

1933—Washington Senators outfielder Heinie Manush got into a bitter dispute with umpire Charley Moran during a World Series game. Manush got so mad that he took hold of Moran's bow tie, which was held on by elastic. Heinie pulled it out a couple of feet and let go. Moran had a terrible time getting enough voice to order Manush out of the game.

III Will

Brooklyn Dodgers pitcher Van Lingle Mungo once got the heave-ho during a 1936 game by umpire Bill Klem.

When reporters later asked the ump why he ejected Mungo, Klem replied, "He wasn't feeling well."

"He looked healthy to us," countered a reporter.

"Well," said Klem, "Mungo told me that he was sick and tired of my stupid decisions."

Terry Francona

Pinch Hitter • Milwaukee, A.L. • July 9, 1989

Terry Francona walked his way into baseball infamy. The Milwaukee Brewer was thrown out of a game after receiving an intentional walk.

It was all because he delivered some ill-timed barbs at plate umpire Ken Kaiser.

The two were involved in a heated argument five weeks earlier in a Brewers–California Angels game when Francona hit a sinking liner to left that Kaiser ruled was caught. Francona protested to no avail, claiming that the ball had been trapped. Subsequent television replays backed him up.

The day of Francona's infamous ejection was Kaiser's first encounter with the Brewers since the disputed play. He was calling balls and strikes at County Stadium in a game between the Brewers and the Baltimore Orioles.

In the top of the sixth inning a foul tip caught Kaiser in the throat. The ump staggered backward, and players from both teams rushed over in fear that he was seriously hurt. At first he couldn't swallow or talk and was taken to the Milwaukee dugout to rest for a few minutes.

Francona, who was still fuming over Kaiser's bad call in the California game, saw his chance to harpoon the umpire, since Kaiser was in no condition to talk back.

"The guys had been teasing me about getting even and were egging me on to go get him," Francona recalled. "So I strolled by while the trainer was working on him and said, 'Now aren't you sorry you screwed up that call? Look what it got you.' He got pissed. I don't blame him, because I didn't know how badly he was hurt. He couldn't even yell at me."

Within a few minutes Kaiser went back behind the plate to finish the game. In the next inning, as luck would have it, Francona was sent up to pinch-hit.

The Orioles elected to intentionally walk him. After Kaiser called the first wide pitch a ball, he growled at Francona, "You're a real comedian. You ought to be in Vegas."

"What do you mean by that?" asked Francona.

"You and your jokes," replied the ump.

The two adversaries began jawing back and forth while the Orioles continued issuing the intentional walk. On ball four Francona tossed his bat and was set to trot down to first when he heard Kaiser say, "I make over 14,000 calls a year, and I don't give a damn about yours."

Retorted Francona, "That's too bad you couldn't make a few of them right."

For that last cutting remark Francona got the thumb. The ejected Brewer really blew his stack, spurring Milwaukee coach Andy Etchebarren to run over and cool him down.

"Careful, careful," Etchebarren cautioned. "You don't want to get thrown out."

"But he already threw me out," said Francona.

"Oh, well, in that case," said the coach, walking away, "go ahead and finish what you were yelling at him."

Rip Sewell

Pitcher • Pittsburgh, N.L. • 1945

Rip Sewell was ejected not only before the game started, but before he even stepped out of the dugout!

The Pittsburgh Pirates pitching ace made the quickest trip to the showers in his 13-year career for insulting the parentage and intelligence of umpire Jocko Conlan, one of the sternest and stuffiest men ever to wear blue.

The heave-ho was the climax of a long-running feud between Sewell and Conlan over the hurler's infamous slider. The pitch broke so sharply when it reached home plate that many believed it was a spitball.

"Jocko and I had been fussing for years," Sewell recalled. "Everyone was always accusing me of throwing spitballs, but Jocko was the worst of all. He couldn't rest easy until he actually caught me with a wet one in my hand."

Whenever Conlan called balls and strikes with Sewell on the mound, the umpire kept the hurler and the Pirates fuming. Conlan would repeatedly stop the game to check for spit on the ball.

"He never could catch me because I never threw a spitter," Sewell insisted. "I threw a slider that broke like a spitter or like a split-fingered fastball. I made a couple of trips to Commissioner Ford Frick's office because I was getting upset over the way people had complained about it."

For Sewell the clincher came during a 1945 game in Philadelphia when Conlan was the second base umpire. "Jocko had been giving me the evil eye all afternoon," the pitcher recalled. "He was in back of me, and this one time he sneaked up from behind just when I went into my windup and he grabbed the ball right out of my hand.

"That's when we really went at it. He was looking for a spitter and there wasn't one bit of spit on that ball."

Even though he lacked evidence, Conlan wasn't convinced Sewell was bone dry, and sent the protesting pitcher to the commissioner's office.

A few days later the adversaries came face to face again, this time in the Pittsburgh dugout before a game. Conlan was passing through from the umpires' dressing room to the field when he spotted Sewell. "Well, Rip, did you and Mr. Frick have a nice visit?" he asked with a sneer.

Sewell crossed his arms, looked Conlan right in the eye, and replied, "Yes, sir. I said, 'Mr. Frick, if I wanted to throw a spitball, I would. But nobody has ever caught me. I'm either the smartest pitcher in baseball or you've got the dumbest umpires.'" Sewell paused for effect and then added, "And you, Jocko, are the dumbest son of a bitch of them all!"

The words had barely tumbled out of Sewell's mouth when Conlan exploded. "You're outta the game!" he bellowed.

Sewell pointed to the field. "The game ain't even started yet, dummy. That just proves my point."

Sewell knew it was useless to argue further. Without another word he headed for the showers.

COACHING CAPERS

◆

It's said that if a retired player wants to drop off the face of the earth, he becomes a coach. During most games, fans don't pay the least bit of attention to the first and third base coaches. However, on rare occasions the coach's box can turn into a stage for some wacky scene-stealing. For "The Zaniest Actions of Coaches," The Baseball Hall of SHAME inducts the following:

Charlie Grimm

Coach • Chicago, N.L. • 1941–43

Charlie Grimm acted more like a stand-up comedian than a first base coach for the Chicago Cubs.

In fact, his antics in the coach's box were so zany that in 1941 the Philadelphia Phillies, in ads promoting an upcoming home game with the Cubs, urged fans to "get a seat behind first base and watch Charlie Grimm coach."

Charlie was Grimm in name only.

After seven years as Cubs manager and two years in the broadcast booth, Grimm staked out the coach's box as a stage to entertain the crowd while directing traffic on the bases.

Once, when a wicked foul line drive nearly beheaded him, Grimm fled from the coach's box and perched himself on the grandstand rail and coached from there.

Another time, after ducking a vicious liner, Grimm called time, ran into the dugout, and returned to the coach's box with a fielder's mitt. He then took his position as though he were one of the infielders.

Jolly Cholly, as he was called, wasn't above poking fun at his own players. In a 1942 game, Cub runner Lou Stringer was almost picked off first base. So Grimm ceremoniously drove an imaginary stake into the ground behind the bag and "tied" Stringer to it. Another time Grimm made a big deal when

Lennie Merullo drew a walk after 16 Cubs in a row had been retired. Grimm staged an elaborate welcoming ceremony at first with a finger whistle. Then he dusted off the bag with his cap and shook hands with the arriving "stranger."

To celebrate a home run by rookie Lou "The Mad Russian" Novikoff, Grimm had the Cubs in the dugout line up in two rows and raise bats to form an arch, under which Grimm ushered Novikoff for a majestic return to the bench.

In his first month as coach, Jolly Cholly learned that his tomfoolery did not extend to umpires. During a spring training game in 1941, umpire Beans Reardon called out a Cub on a bang-bang play at first. Grimm did a perfect backward somersault and returned to his feet with his head in his hands. Reardon warned him that such antics would not be tolerated once the season started.

From then on Grimm avoided antagonizing the arbiters—except once in 1942 at Cincinnati. In that game Grimm was ejected for making fun of an umpire—and it led to one of the strangest official protests in baseball history.

It all started during the second game of a double-header. The Cubs had won the first game 16–1 and were crushing the Reds by another lopsided score in the nightcap.

Irked and restless by this humiliation, the Cincy fans began to boo the Reds and shout uncouth remarks at them. Grimm rushed to the rescue. He began goofing off in the coach's box, diverting fans from their raucous catcalling.

As things calmed down, Grimm glanced around for new material to keep the crowd entertained. He spotted George Barr umpiring behind home plate and began to mimic Barr's strut while the arbiter's back was turned. Suddenly, Barr whirled around, red-faced and red-necked, and, with an inelegant thumb, gave Grimm the old heave-ho.

The fans unleashed a torrent of verbal abuse on the ump and nearly rioted. Cincinnati general manager Warren Giles was so incensed over the ejection that he telegraphed league president Ford Frick protesting Barr's action. Nothing came of the protest other than it was an historic first—a team filing a protest on behalf of a member of the opposing team.

Even when the situation was reversed and his own team was losing big, Jolly Cholly put on a show from the coach's box. In a 1942 game against the Dodgers, the Cubs were trailing 5–0 in the eighth inning. Grimm, in the third base coach's box, pulled the lineup card from his hip pocket and slowly and dramatically tore it into bits. Then he dropped to his hands and knees, dug a little hole in the dirt, and carefully buried the "dead" batting order.

But in the ninth inning the Cubs suddenly broke loose with a belated rally, scoring four runs with only one out and a runner on first. Grimm again dropped to his hands and knees. Furiously, he began to claw at the dirt to salvage the buried and torn scraps of paper. Then he hurriedly tried to piece them back together like a jigsaw puzzle as the crowd roared with laughter.

Before Grimm could reassemble the pieces, the next batter grounded into a game-ending double play—whereupon Jolly Cholly fell over backward in a dead faint.

George Van Haltren

Coach–Center Fielder • New York, N.L. • July 31, 1897

New York Giants player-coach George Van Haltren used a sneaky coaching trick to dupe the opposing pitcher into blowing the game.

Brooklyn Dodgers hurler Brickyard Kennedy had baffled the Giants throughout the day. He had fashioned a three-hit shutout going into the top of the ninth with Brooklyn ahead 2–0. The last thing Van Haltren wanted to see was Brickyard recording his first whitewash of the crosstown rivals.

As the Giants fans began filtering out of the ballpark, leadoff batter Jouett

Meekin lined a clean single. Then Van Haltren, who played center field and was also the third base coach, left his coaching post to bat. He whacked a single, moving Meekin to third.

An error on Mike Tiernan's grounder brought in New York's first run, and a sacrifice bunt put Van Haltren on third and Tiernan on second. An infield hit by George Davis tied the score as Van Haltren crossed the plate and then returned to the third base coach's box. The Giants now had the winning run on third, an insurance run on first, and only one out.

Throwing with all his might, Kennedy blazed two fastballs past batter Kid Gleason. The hurler thought he caught the corner on the next pitch for strike three, but umpire Hank O'Day called it a ball. Brickyard blew his stack and spewed a string of epithets that nearly got him the thumb.

On the next pitch Gleason lofted a sacrifice fly, driving in Tiernan with the go-ahead run and moving Davis to second base. Kennedy and his catcher, John Grim, then exploded and took their wrath out on O'Day for his call on the previous pitch. But time had never been called.

The scheming Van Haltren thought this was the perfect time to steal a run with a clever ruse. While Grim had his back to the pitcher and was arguing with O'Day, and Kennedy was shouting invectives from the mound, Van Haltren made a mad dash for the plate, even though he wasn't a runner.

Brickyard, seeing nothing but a Giant trying to steal home, fired the ball to the plate. But Grim was still arguing with O'Day, and the ball sailed past the catcher and rolled all the way to the backstop. Meanwhile, Davis, the real runner on second, scampered around third and raced home with the fourth tally of the inning.

That proved to be the winning run, as Brooklyn scored only one run in the bottom of the ninth. Thanks to the coach's con, the Dodgers lost 4–3.

Hughie Jennings

Manager • Detroit, A.L. • 1907

Detroit Tigers manager Hughie Jennings was once ejected from a game because he rattled the opposition with an annoyingly shrill policeman's whistle.

While Jennings was piloting the Tigers, he often coached at third base, where he developed a special ear-piercing shriek designed to irk the opposing team. It sounded like a loud, high-pitched "eee-yah!" which irritated the eardrums and jangled the nerves.

During a series with the Boston Red Sox in 1907, Jennings was afflicted with a bad case of laryngitis and couldn't even let out a squeak, much to the relief of the Boston players and fans. Jennings went through one day of maddening silence and couldn't stand it. He just had to find a way to make noise. As he left the ball park, he spotted a policeman who was blowing his whistle while chasing a suspect.

"That's it!" Jennings said. He went straight to the police station and finagled a cop out of his whistle.

The next afternoon Jennings began blowing the shrill policeman's whistle from the coach's box. It sounded even more infuriating than his patented shriek.

Finally, Boston manager Deacon McGuire appealed to umpire Silk O'Loughlin to silence the aggravating whistle. The ump agreed, and marched over to Jennings. "Put that damn whistle away," ordered the ump. "It's driving us all crazy."

But Jennings took a defiant stance. "Kindly show me anything in the rule book that says it's illegal to toot on a policeman's whistle," Jennings said smugly. Then he kept right on blowing the whistle.

"Well, Hughie, let me show you something," countered the umpire. He gave a dramatic sweep of his thumb, the unmistakable gesture of ejection. "And I'll throw you out again tomorrow and the next day and any other game that you try to use that damn whistle."

Jennings pleaded to American League president Ban Johnson for a ruling in his favor, but Johnson sided with the umpire.

But Jennings got in the last toot. He practiced a high-decibel whistle by blowing with two fingers in his mouth. It was just as ear-splitting as the policeman's whistle. From then on Jennings alternated using his new natural whistle with his old, obnoxious "eee-yah!"

And there was nothing the umpires could do about it.

Burt Shotton

Third Base Coach • Cleveland, A.L. • 1945

Burt Shotton made a great play by spearing a line drive. The only problem was, he was coaching third base at the time—and he put out his own man to retire the side!

Shotton coached for the Cleveland Indians in the mid-1940s. But he never quite got over his playing days in the outfield from 1909–23 while on the St. Louis Browns and later the Cardinals. Burt still had the urge to catch anything hit his way. He always had this fielding itch under control—except once.

During a 1945 game against the Chicago White Sox at Comiskey Park, the Indians were trailing by a run in the top of the seventh inning with two out. Cleveland first baseman Mickey Rocco, who had a habit of getting rallies started, stepped up to the plate. However, any chance to ignite a rally in the frame vanished when Rocco cracked a soft foul liner down the third base line.

White Sox third baseman Tony Cuccinello darted over in foul territory, hoping to snare the ball. But Shotton was in a much better position to make the play. Like the fielder he used to be, the old coach reached out and snagged the liner with one hand. Then, triumphantly, he fired the ball back to the astonished Chicago pitcher.

"I almost yelled, 'Nice catch, Burt!' " recalled Cleveland manager Lou Boudreau. "But then I remembered whose side he was on, and my next reaction was to just ignore it and hope nobody else noticed that what he did was wrong."

Unfortunately for the Indians, Chicago skipper Jimmy Dykes had indeed noticed. He came bouncing out of the dugout crying foul over the foul catch. And while Shotton sheepishly dug his toe in the dirt, the umpire ruled that since Cuccinello had a chance to make the catch, Shotton was guilty of interference. As a result, the ump called Rocco out to end the inning.

"As far as I know," Boudreau said, "that's the only time a coach ever put out his own man."

Nick Altrock

Coach • Washington, A.L. • July 28, 1912

Third base coach Nick Altrock helped his team win a game by making the opposing pitcher laugh himself silly.

Just days earlier, Altrock, a former player with a rubbery face and a hilarious wit, was hired by Washington Senators manager Clark Griffith to coach. "Put some life into this club," the skipper told him. "I've never seen such a deadpan gang in all my life."

Altrock took his comedy seriously. In a game against the Cleveland Indians, the Senators held a slim 1–0 lead when Altrock decided to put on a big act in the coach's box to distract Cleveland pitcher Vean Gregg.

As Gregg was pitching to Chick Gandil, Altrock began boxing with himself. He dodged and weaved as he tried to jab and punch himself. Players doubled up in laughter. Gregg stopped pitching and looked on with bemused fascination while the crowd roared in hysterics and rattled their seats over Altrock's crazy antics.

Gregg broke out in uncontrollable laughter when Altrock knocked himself down, staggered back to his feet, and then launched into a solo wrestling bout. By now Gregg was holding his heaving sides as the double-jointed jester in the coach's box tied himself up in a half nelson and threw himself on his back after a desperate struggle.

The laughing fit left Gregg so weak, he fell to his knees on the mound. Finally, umpire Fred Westervelt decided to put a stop to the clowning. He started walking over to Altrock, but halfway there, Westervelt's stomach muscles contracted so violently from laughing that he couldn't talk. When he

regained control, he told Altrock, "You sure are a hoot, Nick. But I have to ask you to quit this act. We've got a game to play, and your cutups just aren't in keeping with the dignity of an American League game."

Altrock reluctantly agreed. But he accomplished what he set out to do. Gregg simply couldn't concentrate on the batters. Just when he was set to pitch, he'd begin to giggle and break out into a guffaw. He quickly gave up eight more hits and three more runs and lost the game 4–1.

Afterward, Cleveland manager Joe Birmingham protested to American League president Ban Johnson and demanded that Altrock be permanently banned from putting on a comedy act from the coach's box.

Johnson traveled to Cleveland the next day to watch the comic coach in action. Recalled Altrock, "I outdid myself. I put on the funniest skit of my life and I had Ban laughing harder than anybody else. That night, he put the okay on Nick Altrock as a comedian, but he did ask me not to stage my stuff while play actually was going on.

"However, my act did spell the end of Vean Gregg, and it won the game for us."

PRANKS A LOT!

◆

They are the cards of baseball—all jokers. They pull off more pranks than double plays. They throw more bull than fastballs. And they often catch more flak than pop flies. No teammate, no manager, no front office executive is safe from being victimized by these audacious pranksters. For "The Most Madcap Jokesters," The Baseball Hall of SHAME inducts the following:

Jim Colborn

Pitcher • Chicago, N.L.; Milwaukee-Kansas City-Seattle, A.L.
1969–78

Jim Colborn was an incurable impersonator who often masqueraded as an umpire, team mascot, groundskeeper, peanut vendor, or ball boy—usually while the game was still going on.

Colborn launched his career as an impostor during a 1975 game when he pitched for the Milwaukee Brewers. Back then the stadium grounds crew wore bright yellow lederhosen—Bavarian costumes with short pants and long socks that came up to the knees. After the top of the fifth inning, the crew would race out onto the diamond and drag the infield.

"I put on one of their outfits and ran out with them," recalled Colborn. "It took a few minutes for the fans to catch on. I don't think anyone would have noticed, except that dumb outfit made me look like a sick canary. When they started laughing, [Brewers manager] Del Crandall realized it was me and he yelled at me to get my ass off the field. He was really fuming when I ran into the dugout. But he took one look at me in that outfit with my bony knees exposed and he cracked up.

"After that, it became kind of a tradition to pull off something like that. The guys expected me to do something outrageous."

The following year Colborn hoodwinked the Brewers' new skipper, Alex

Grammas, when Jim masqueraded as an umpire for the lineup exchange before the last game of the season. Colborn wore a maroon blazer and gray pants like the umpires. He donned a mask and chest protector and strolled out to home plate with the arbiters, who were in on the gag.

"I carried the game ball and went through the lineup exchange with [Detroit Tigers manager] Ralph Houk and Grammas," Colborn recalled. "Then I said, 'Have a nice winter, Alex.' He gave me a glance, went back to talking to Ralph, then did a great double take and yelled, 'What the hell are you doing out here?'"

Colborn then marched to the Brewers dugout and ejected all the bench jockeys who were giving him a hard time. "I really did it as a favor," he insisted. "Since it was the last game of the season, they wanted to go home early. But the ejections didn't stick. I tried to throw myself out, too, but it didn't work either."

Another time, Colborn dressed up as the team mascot, Bernie Brewer. Whenever the Brewers hit a homer or pulled off a spectacular play, Bernie Brewer slid down a chute in the center-field stands into a giant mug and set loose a shower of balloons to simulate foam. "I went down the chute during a game," recalled Colborn. "Everybody on the team, except the manager, knew I was going to do it. They cheered me on. You can tell we really paid a lot of attention to playing baseball in those days."

Before being traded to the Kansas City Royals, Jim pulled off a prank at the expense of retiring superstar Henry Aaron.

"They were having a special night for Henry," said Colborn. "The governor was there along with the baseball commissioner, the owner of the team, Mickey Mantle, Willie Mays, and a whole bunch of people. They were presenting Henry with all these fabulous gifts.

"Just before the presentations were over, I got Bob Uecker, who was master of ceremonies, to announce that the team got Henry a new car. Then I drove out from under the stands in this terrible old wreck that I bought at a demolition derby the night before for five dollars. Henry was speechless."

Jim continued his impersonations with the Kansas City Royals. One time he sat in for the ball boy on the first base foul line and played catch with the California Angels' Bobby Bonds between innings. "Bobby didn't realize who I was at first," said Colborn. "When he finally recognized me, he got mad because I had struck him out the previous day. So then he tried to bean me."

Jim ended his career as a major league pitcher and impostor with the Seattle Mariners in 1978. Colborn capped off his final day in the bigs in typical fashion—by selling peanuts in the Kingdome stands.

Pepper Martin

Pepper Martin raised hell for fun, not sin.

He was the spiritual leader of the "Gas House Gang"—a rollicking, wild group of St. Louis Cardinals who played hard on the field and even harder off it.

The Oklahoma-born "Wild Hoss of the Osage" acted like a devilish boy who never grew up. He was a high-spirited jokester who pulled pranks when he was cold sober and old enough to know better. To him, every day was a belly laugh.

He discovered that hotel lobbies were perfect places for playing jokes. Anytime the stuffed shirts in the lobby of a swank hotel began to sneeze, his teammates knew that Pepper had scattered sneezing powder.

Martin liked to lean out of his upper-story hotel window and toss water bombs at unsuspecting pedestrians on the sidewalk below. His targets were often reporters, hotel guests, and even his own manager.

One day on the road, Pepper filled a bag with water and dropped it from his fifth-floor hotel window. He made a direct hit on St. Louis manager Frankie Frisch, who was returning to the hotel in a new suit.

After bombing Frisch, Martin raced down five flights of stairs and streaked to a chair in the hotel lobby and began reading a newspaper. Seconds later the dripping-wet Frisch walked in the door. The miffed manager stared at the innocent-looking Martin and said, "I can't believe it. I could have sworn it was you who threw that water on me."

Sometimes when lobby-sitting bored him, Pepper staged a fake fight with a teammate, who pretended to hit him in the face. Popcorn fell out of Pepper's mouth like dislodged teeth and ketchup dripped from his lips like blood. Women guests shrieked until Martin broke up laughing.

In one of his most memorable pranks, Martin and teammate Rip Collins dressed as workmen and barged into a convention banquet at the Bellevue Stratford Hotel in Philadelphia. They threw the place into an uproar as they moved around the tables and discussed plans for redecorating the room. The charade ended when the hotel manager arrived, recognized the zany Cardinals, and introduced them to the rattled banquet crowd.

Pepper was a master put-on artist. One afternoon at the Chase Hotel he and the team's batboy, YoYo, sat on the lobby floor next to a large plant. Pepper then sliced a loaf of bread and clipped off some leaves from the plant.

After spreading the leaves and mustard on the bread, he and YoYo ate the sandwiches while the hotel guests stared in wide-eyed amazement. "Why, you folks act like you never seen a feller have lunch before," he said to the growing crowd. "Or maybe you never ate this kinda food. Like to have a bite?" When no one took up his offer, he added, "There's plenty more good dishes where this comes from." Turning to YoYo, he said, "Tell the folks your favorite recipe."

"Chrysanthemums," said YoYo between mouthfuls of leaves, bread, and mustard. "But if you ever try it, you oughter mix in a rose petal or two and don't fergit the pickle. Rose petals need pickles to spice 'em up."

Since he loved music, Martin formed the baseball world's wackiest band—the Mississippi Musical Mudcats. Its members were all Cardinals. With Pepper as bandleader, Frenchy Bordagaray played the washboard, Bob Weiland the jug, Bill McGee the fiddle, and Lon Warneke the guitar. The Mudcats, who specialized in hoedown music, entertained guests in hotel lobbies, fans in the stands, and fellow passengers on trains.

The band played for fun wherever it could find a crowd. "And now, ladies and gentlemen," Pepper would announce, "the Musical Mudcats will present that gripping classic of the hills, 'Willie, My Toes Are So Cold,' followed by 'They Buried My Sweetie Under an Old Pine Tree.' " After their performance, he would pass the hat. Anything for a laugh.

Once, when the Mudcats were practicing in the clubhouse, in walked owner Sam Breadon, who believed players should keep their minds solely on baseball. Rather than wait for a stern lecture from Breadon, Pepper marched over to him and said in a firm manner, "Mr. Breadon, I want it understood that none of the Mudcats is to be sold or traded this season. You can't expect us to build up a fine musical organization and have you ruin it. It isn't fair to us and it isn't fair to art."

Although Martin did most of his cutting up off the field, he occasionally had fun during the game. One afternoon when the temperature in St. Louis soared to a sizzling 110 degrees, Pepper and teammate Dizzy Dean gathered scraps of paper and pieces of wood and built a fire in front of the dugout. Then they wrapped themselves in some Navajo blankets and mocked the blazing sun by squatting Indian style in front of the fire while the crowd roared with laughter.

Martin once nearly gave his manager Frankie Frisch a heart attack. Pepper, playing third, had a sudden urge for a chew of tobacco. Even though a batsman was up, Martin didn't bother calling time. He simply removed his glove, tucked it under his arm, and reached into his hip pocket for his cut plug. Just then the batter drilled a sharp shot toward third. There was Pepper—glove under his armpit and a cut plug in his teeth. So he leaned forward and let the speeding ball bounce off his chest. Then he leisurely picked up the ball and fired to first to get his man.

"I almost busted a blood vessel getting Pepper to forget his damned tobacco and pay attention to the game," recalled Frisch. "The guy was either nuts—or a genius. Maybe both."

Shamefully Funny Pranks

1988—When actor Tom Selleck took batting practice with the Baltimore Orioles, Minnesota Twins infielder Al Newman asked him for an autograph. But Selleck brushed him off. So Newman took a white towel, filled it with shaving cream, and got Baltimore's Cal Ripken to hand the sabotaged towel to Selleck, who then unknowingly spread shaving cream all over his face.

1988—Teammates of St. Louis Cardinals hurler Joe Magrane had somebody from Chicago call him and say that *Gentleman's Quarterly* wanted to do a photo feature on him. Magrane was told to come to the ballpark with six winter outfits for a photo shoot. Magrane posed in such apparel as three-piece suits and sweaters, even though it was 105 degrees on the field. After an hour of sweating in the sweltering heat, he received a telegram that read, "Due to your subpar season, we've decided not to use your session in *GQ*." The next day he got another telegram, which read, "Roses are red, violets are blue. You've been had. There is no *GQ*."

1980—Before a spring training game, Los Angeles Dodgers utility man Mickey Hatcher sneaked into the clubhouse, stole manager Tommy Lasorda's pants, cut them apart, and ran them up a flagpole in center field.

1979—During a game in Philadelphia's Veterans Stadium, Pittsburgh Pirates catcher Ed Ott used a portable john in the bullpen in the last inning. His teammates then turned the john over on its door so Ott couldn't get out. He was left there for 30 minutes before being rescued.

1978—Los Angeles Dodgers relief pitcher Terry Forster decided to get even with Davey Lopes, who had pulled some pranks on him. Forster used the number from one of Lopes's credit cards to order $400 worth of porno-graphic magazines. "He was getting them for weeks," Forster recalled. "I had them delivered to the ball park, and it had to be embarrassing opening those things up at the stadium. He had no idea where they were coming from."

Rabbit Maranville

Shortstop • Boston-Pittsburgh-Chicago-Brooklyn-St. Louis, N.L.
1912–35

Rabbit Maranville was baseball's imp.

The five-foot, five-inch Hall of Fame shortstop had a huge appetite for the ludicrous. He acted on every zany impulse, from diving fully clothed into a hotel goldfish pond to filling up a hotel closet with pigeons.

A master prankster, Rabbit had teammates entertained . . . and often enraged.

In 1920 he started a playful wrestling match with Boston Braves teammate Jack Scott in a hotel room filled with fellow players. "Stay away from me, Rabbit," warned the six-foot, three-inch, 200-pound Scott. "I don't want to wrestle you because I might hurt you."

The shortstop responded by charging Scott, who then reluctantly applied a headlock that sent Maranville slumping to the floor in a dead faint. Before leaving the room, Scott, a religious man, said, "Lord, forgive me. I sure didn't want to hurt that boy."

When Maranville recovered, he conjured up a cruel trick. He smeared talcum powder on his face and arms and stretched out in bed like a corpse. Then he sent a teammate to tell Scott that Rabbit was dead. Scott raced to the room, fell to his knees in front of Maranville's bed, and prayed fervently for a miracle to restore the little shortstop's life. "Lord, you know I didn't mean that boy any harm," he prayed. "Please put the breath of life back into the Rabbit. Please, Lord, have mercy on me—and him—and let the little Rabbit live."

The dazed Scott then went down to the lobby, sat in a chair, and awaited the arrival of the police to pick him up on a murder rap. He was still there early the next morning when Maranville strolled blithely by and said, "Hello, Jack. My, you're up early." When Scott recovered from the shock, he was ready to commit real murder.

During a 1922 road trip, when he was with the Pittsburgh Pirates, Rabbit and teammate Chief Yellowhorse shared a suite with manager Bill McKechnie at the Ansonia Hotel in New York. McKechnie wanted to keep an eye on his two "wild Indians." Returning from an evening movie, the manager was surprised to see both players asleep. So he undressed very quietly. Then he opened the closet—and a flock of pigeons flew into his face and nearly toppled him. "Rabbit!" McKechnie thundered. "What's going on?"

Maranville blinked and said, "Those are the Chief's pigeons. Don't open the other closet door or mine will fly out, too."

Maranville was fearless. During a rainout in Philadelphia in 1930, some of the Braves started a poker game at the Majestic Hotel. Rabbit wanted to play, but they wouldn't let him because of his penchant for deliberately screwing up games. So the poker players shoved Rabbit out of the hotel room, locked the door, and started dealing out the cards.

About 30 minutes later one of the players emitted a cry of horror. The Rabbit was looking in from the outside of the hotel window—ten stories above the street! He had climbed out in the rain onto a narrow ledge and worked his way around a corner and across several hundred feet to get to the window. The players immediately opened up the window and let the sopping-wet Rabbit join in their game.

Maranville got a charge out of shocking people—especially hotel guests. He occasionally took dives into the fountain in the courtyard of the Buckingham Hotel in St. Louis when he was fully clothed, just so he could catch some goldfish with his hands—and eat the fish live.

His pranks often took courage. During spring training in Los Angeles, he and Detroit Tigers infielder Fred Haney hopped on a little two-car train that ran from the harbor to downtown. Seeing there were no seats left, Maranville told Haney, "If you've got the guts, I can get us the seats."

Rabbit moved over to where he had spotted a motorman's cap and put it on. Then he announced, "Ladies and gentlemen, only the front car of this train is going into town." Those in the rear car moved to the front and the two players had the car all to themselves. But soon the crowd in the front noticed that the rear car was still attached. The passengers began advancing on the two players. That's when the Rabbit told Haney, "Now here's where the guts come in."

Al Schacht

Pitcher • Washington, A.L. • 1919–21

From the very beginning, scouts, managers, owners, and even fans knew that Al Schacht had the potential to make it big, really big, in the major leagues.

He blossomed into a superstar all right; not as the next Cy Young, but as the Clown Prince of Baseball.

From the 1920s through the 1960s the former sore-armed hurler tickled the ribs of millions of fans in virtually every major and minor league ball park with his hilarious pregame comedy routines.

Long before he became strictly an entertainer, Schacht made fans laugh with his antics on the field, especially in the minors, where he built a reputation as a baseball zany.

For instance, during a 1913 International League game against Buffalo, Schacht conjured up the wackiest version ever of the hidden-ball trick. In the game, Schacht, the Newark pitcher, drew a walk. It was the first time he had reached base in six games, prompting an old Newark fan to shout, "Mister Al, that there is virgin territory. Don't you wander none."

Schacht turned to holler something back, when the opposing pitcher fired to first in an effort to pick him off. The throw, low and wide, hit Schacht on the hip and then rolled underneath him. The first baseman frantically searched for the ball but couldn't find it. Trying to confuse the opposing team, the Newark fan then yelled, "It's in the bullpen!" Meanwhile, Schacht slipped the ball into his own hip pocket and took off for a romp around the bases.

Pandemonium broke out among the Buffalo players as they scrambled all over the field looking desperately for the ball. Schacht kept right on running

until he had slid triumphantly across the plate. But his slide had jarred the ball loose and sent it trickling to the feet of umpire Bill O'Brien.

"Out!" shouted the umpire.

"Aw, I was only fooling," said Schacht.

"Well, I'm not," replied the no-nonsense arbiter. "You're out for interference. And I'm going to report you to the league president."

Schacht was fined $50 by league president Ed Barrow for making a mockery of the game. From then on people began taking note of Schacht more for his pranks than his pitching.

During another game, Schacht found a ten-cent baseball known as a "rocket." Made of tightly pressed rags with an oilcloth cover, the ball had about as much bounce as a rolled-up pair of socks. Schacht stuck it in his back pocket. When he entered the game as a relief pitcher, he swapped an official league ball for the rocket. Neither the umpire nor the opposing team suspected anything was wrong.

Schacht threw the rocket right down the pipe to the first batter, who struck a blow that should have carried the ball into the next county. But the ball, now slightly misshapen from being hit, wobbled weirdly on the fly to the shortstop. Schacht rubbed up the ball to make it round again. Then the next batter also connected solidly with the ball, only to pop it up to Schacht. When the third batter, rival pitcher Rube Parnham, made solid contact, the ball rolled crazily to Schacht, who tagged him out.

"Lemme see that ball!" demanded Parnham. Schacht deftly switched balls again and threw him the official hardball. The blazing mad Parnham took one look and then flung the ball over the grandstand roof. For this startling outburst, Parnham was ejected.

Schacht outdid himself during a 1914 game against Buffalo. Shortly before he was scheduled to pitch, he was outside the ballpark where he spotted a horse-drawn cab with a driver in a tuxedo and top hat. Schacht had a brilliant idea. He paid the cabbie and then launched his prank.

When it was time to pitch, Schacht entered through the outfield gate—on horseback! Not only that, but he was clad in top hat and tails. Howls of laughter shook the ball park as Schacht and the horse made their way to the mound. After leaving a smelly memento on the mound, the horse was led away, and Schacht, still in his finery, began pitching.

But it was simply too cumbersome to pitch in formal attire. He got knocked out of the box in the third inning. The next day, Jack Yellon, a sportswriter for the *Buffalo Courier,* became the first to call Schacht the "Clown Prince of Baseball." The name stuck.

It took a prank by Schacht to finally make it to the majors. After every shutout victory that he pitched in 1919 for last-place Newark, Schacht clipped the newspaper account of the game and mailed it with a letter to Clark Griffith, owner of the Washington Senators. The wording of each letter was always the same. It read:

Dear Sir,

Enclosed you will find a clipping of Al Schacht's work. He is without doubt the best pitcher in the International League. I happened to see him pitch all his shutouts this season, and if he were with a good club, he'd have several more. As I used to be in baseball myself, I think I know a pitcher when I see one. Why don't you get wise to yourself and get this fellow?

Yours truly,
Just a fan

Intrigued by this steady stream of mail, Griffith went to Newark near the end of the year and watched Schacht pitch his tenth shutout of the season. Griffith bought him that night and brought him back to Washington, where Schacht won the only two games he started that year.

It wasn't until ten years later that Griffith learned he had been conned by Schacht. But by then all he could do was laugh.

THE NOT SO FINE PRINT

♦

An amazing thing happens when management discusses contracts. Players are worth so very much on the trading block, yet worth so very little during salary negotiations. When contract talks stall, some players fold up. Others hold out. And most players strike out more often in the front office than on the diamond. For "The Most Outlandish Contractual Disputes," The Baseball Hall of SHAME inducts the following:

Dale Mitchell

Outfielder • Cleveland, A.L.; Brooklyn, N.L. • 1946–56

Dale Mitchell held out longer than any other player in major league history—seven years!

He was an exciting new hitting prospect who turned into a determined veteran holdout. Unfortunately, by the time he gave in and reached the majors, he was past his prime.

In 1939, when Dale was a 17-year-old high school junior in Oklahoma, Cleveland Indians scout Hugh Alexander offered a bonus to Mitchell if he would sign a Cleveland contract. Dale knew his family needed the money badly because his father was in poor health and the medical bills were piling up.

As a signing bonus, Alexander promised Mitchell a regular monthly allowance until he was ready to enter the minors when he graduated. Dale and his parents agreed to the terms and his parents signed the contract. But the deal had to be kept secret; otherwise, Mitchell would have been ineligible to play high school sports.

The Mitchells made a crucial mistake. They accepted Alexander's word that they would receive monthly payments. However, there was no mention of any bonus payments in the contract. As a result, they never received the money.

Alexander made an honest effort to back his promise, but someone in the Indians front office squelched the bonus plan because it wasn't in the contract.

When Dale graduated in 1940, the Indians ordered him to report to one of their minor league farm teams. But Mitchell refused. Feeling that the Tribe had reneged on the bonus, he tore up every piece of mail they sent him. The club tried other approaches—by phone, even by personal appeals. Dale insisted that he wouldn't listen until Cleveland made good on the bonus. And so began baseball's longest holdout.

Meanwhile, Mitchell was forced to spurn numerous other scouts. Because the Cleveland contract had been signed, he couldn't legally sign another. Neither could he tell the scouts the real reason why he turned them down, for fear he would be ineligible for college baseball.

Since he couldn't reach agreement with Cleveland, Dale enrolled at the University of Oklahoma, where he played baseball for two years until he was drafted by the armed forces. Returning to school after nearly three years overseas with the Army Air Force, Mitchell sparked the Oklahoma team with an amazing .507 batting average in 1946.

Again the scouts hounded him. Again Dale had to reject them. His holdout period had now extended through seven long years, and it looked like it would go on forever. Mitchell was now a 24-year-old husband and father who had yet to play one inning of professional baseball, while players his age were nearing the peak of their major league careers.

Then one day Dale read that the Indians had reached a working agreement with Oklahoma City, a team in the AA Texas League. He visited the club's owners, Harold Pope and Jim Humphries, and told them his tale of woe. They listened sympathetically. They worked out an arrangement with the Indians whereby the Tribe would assign Mitchell to Oklahoma City so he could be close to home and finish his schooling during the off-season. The deal hinged on whether Dale would end his record-setting holdout. Knowing this was his last chance, Mitchell agreed.

On June 3, 1946—more than seven years after that first Cleveland contract—Dale made his pro debut. He went hitless in his first game, but the next night collected three hits. He wound up winning the Texas League batting title with an average of .337.

The Indians were so impressed, they brought him up to the majors at the end of the 1946 season. To make sure the Tribe wouldn't slight Mitchell, Pope and Humphries accompanied their star to Cleveland. They told club president Bill Veeck the reason for Dale's unequaled holdout was the financial runaround the Indians had given him.

Veeck quickly made amends. "I couldn't let the world's record for determination go unrewarded," said Veeck as he handed Mitchell a check for the long-sought-after bonus.

The 25-year-old rookie responded by batting .432 in the club's final 11 games. He went on to play 11 seasons, all but one with Cleveland, and finished with an impressive lifetime batting average of .312. Had he not held out for seven years and started so late, who knows how great a hitter Dale Mitchell might have become.

Turkey Mike Donlin

Outfielder • St. Louis-Cincinnati-New York-Boston-Pittsburgh, N.L.; Baltimore, A.L. • 1899–1908, 1911–12, 1914

Because of a contract dispute, hitting star Turkey Mike Donlin deserted baseball at the peak of his career for a new life in vaudeville.

National Baseball Library

But then, following a two-year holdout, when Donlin tried to make a comeback on the diamond, he flopped—just as he had on the stage.

Turkey Mike—who earned his nickname because he trotted like a turkey and had a big red neck—was one of the leading hitters in the National League during the first decade of the century. In 1908 he batted .334 for the New York Giants, the eighth time in nine years that he had hit over .300.

After that season Donlin was bitten by both the love bug and the acting bug. He met a young vaudeville actress named Mabel Hite and, following a whirlwind courtship, married her. Then the two began performing on the stage together.

When his baseball contract for the next season arrived, Turkey Mike sent it back demanding a $1,500 raise, to $8,000. The Giants refused, so he told them that until they met his demands, he'd play in the theater, not on the diamond.

His holdout lasted two full years, much to the dismay of his fans. They wanted so desperately to see him back with the Giants that they began chanting a ditty at the Polo Grounds:

If Donlin would only join the Giants,
The fans would drink his health in pints.

They sang it until Donlin caved in and returned to the Giants in 1911. But he was out of condition and the footlights had dimmed his batting eye. "Turkey Mike has been dancing the boards with his wife for two seasons, but he still does the turkey trot when he walks on the diamond," sniped *The New York Times*. The Giants sold him to Boston, who traded him to Pittsburgh. After playing sparingly in 1912, Turkey Mike could not come to terms with his new team, the Philadelphia Phillies, so he returned to the stage.

Certain well-meaning producers starred Mike and his wife in a legitimate play, but it closed shortly after it opened because the critics panned it. The next year, Mrs. Donlin died. On her deathbed she urged Turkey Mike to go back to baseball.

Determined to make good again, he played minor league ball in 1913. The following year Donlin tried a comeback with the Giants, who used him exclusively as a pinch hitter. His job was to come to the plate with the game in the balance. This pleased Turkey Mike's sense of the dramatic, but, unfortunately, he was then no greater a batter than he was an actor. He hit .161 in 31 games before he was given his unconditional release.

Donlin was never more than a bit actor the rest of his life.

Benny "Earache" Meyer

Outfielder • Brooklyn, N.L. • 1913

Benny Meyer used a lot of bull, literally, to hoodwink Brooklyn Dodgers owner Charles Ebbets into giving him a better contract.

Months before the start of the 1913 season, the Dodgers sent Meyer a contract calling for $2,400 for the year. That wasn't bad money in those days, but it wasn't good either. So Meyer decided to do something about it.

As a favor, a friend of his in the printing business made up some fancy letterhead stationery for the "Bernhard Meyer Stock Farm." On this letterhead, Meyer sent a polite note to the Dodgers stating that there was no way he could leave his Missouri stock farm to play baseball for so small a salary as $2,400. He said it would cost him much more than that just to hire someone to operate his huge farm. So, unless the Dodgers could see their way clear to upping the ante by plenty, Benny regrettably would have to decline the offer and stay home all summer.

Of course, this was all pure bull. Benny didn't have a big stock farm. He only had a few acres out back of his Ozark home, where he kept a couple of cows.

The letter produced some unexpected results. When Ebbets, the Dodgers owner, read it, he put a lot of stock in Meyer's note. The owner wrote back that he was interested in cattle himself and had decided to visit Benny's farm. Ebbets said he would arrive in three weeks. And incidentally, he added, while he was there they could discuss the contract.

When Meyer received the letter, he nearly fell off his chair. This was not what he had planned. But Benny, with the guts of a bunco man, was determined to bamboozle the team owner. Meyer called on his friends and neighbors for help. They loaned him all of their cattle and helped him build an impressive sign extolling the merits of the "Bernhard Meyer Stock Farm."

When Ebbets arrived, Benny showed him his immense stock farm. He failed to mention that most of the land and almost all the livestock belonged to his neighbors. Ebbets was duly impressed. Believing that Meyer could indeed ill afford to leave the farm on such a small baseball salary, Ebbets gave him the contract he wanted.

Branch Rickey

General Manager • St. Louis, N.L. • 1932

Few players who wrangled over their contracts with Branch Rickey ever came away winners. He could negotiate the socks off a Teamster. He often had good players and enough money—he just didn't like to see the two of them mix.

"Branch didn't like to pay out money," said one of his best players, Enos Slaughter. "He'd go into the vault to get you a nickel change."

Woe be to those players foolish enough to dicker with him over salaries. If he couldn't beat them with tough talk, he'd beat them with flimflam. That's what he did to St. Louis Cardinals relief pitcher Jim Lindsey.

Before the start of spring training in 1932, Rickey sent Lindsey a proposed contract that contained figures the pitcher didn't like. Despite Rickey's deserved reputation as a tough, tightfisted negotiator, Lindsey decided to take on the general manager one on one. So Lindsey traveled from his home in Louisiana to St. Louis to haggle.

In Rickey's office, Lindsey presented his case for a raise, which centered on his record the previous year—6 wins, 4 losses, 7 saves, and a 2.77 ERA.

When it was Rickey's turn to talk, Lindsey didn't try to rebut him. He merely sat in the chair and kept repeating, "I want more money."

Negotiations were deadlocked when Rickey decided to pull off a dirty little trick. He left the room for a few minutes to set up a sneaky hoax, and then returned for more contract discussions.

Within a minute his phone rang. Rickey grabbed it and said, "Rochester calling? . . . Put them on. . . . Yes . . . You need pitchers? Right-handed pitchers . . . Well, I don't know. . . . We're a little short right now, but I'll see what I can do."

Hanging up from the call, Rickey resumed bargaining with Lindsey until he was interrupted by another call. "Columbus calling? . . . Put them on. . . . You need help in the bullpen? . . . I'll get someone down there in time to start spring training with you."

After Rickey hung up, Lindsey had the look of a poker player who was folding with two pair. In a voice filled with resignation, the hurler told Rickey, "Gimme your contract. I'll sign it. I don't know whether or not you're kidding, but I can't afford to take the chance."

Joe Corbett

Pitcher • Baltimore, N.L. • 1897

Baltimore Orioles pitcher Joe Corbett stayed out of baseball for six years because his manager welched on a bet.

Before the beginning of the 1897 season, Corbett, who in two previous seasons had a 3–2 record, made a bet with manager Ned Hanlon that if the hurler won 20 games, the skipper would buy him a $40 suit.

That year Corbett pitched his heart out and, to everyone's surprise, won 24 games.

After his 20th win, Corbett asked Hanlon to pay up. But the manager kept putting off the payment, more as a cruel joke than anything else. He wanted to string Corbett along for as long as he could.

But Hanlon overestimated Corbett's patience and sense of humor. For the rest of the season the hurler fretted about his manager's refusal to honor the bet. Finally, Corbett walked into Hanlon's office and said, "If you don't pay up, then I have no respect for what you say. And if I can't respect you, I can't play for you. So here's the rub. If you don't come through, then I'm through."

Hanlon, who didn't believe any player could get so steamed over a $40 bet that he would quit the game, ignored Corbett's threat. Figuring that he could rattle the pitcher just a little while longer, the manager said, "Well, if you feel that way about it, go ahead. Quit."

But Hanlon's questionable joke got way out of hand. The sensitive Corbett left for his home in San Francisco for the winter, still not knowing that Hanlon was putting him on.

The manager figured he'd pay up the following spring. But when the Orioles offered Corbett his new contract, he turned it down. In fact, he rejected every offer the team made and told the Orioles that he would never pitch for them again. That was no joke.

Corbett never did pitch for them or anyone else over the next six years. Finally, in 1904, he joined the St. Louis Cardinals, and after a lackluster year, retired from the game without ever getting his new suit.

As for ever playing for Ned Hanlon again, Joe Corbett found him just too "unsuitable."

Rube Waddell

Pitcher • Philadelphia, A.L. • 1904

Rube Waddell, the eccentric pitcher for the Philadelphia Athletics, refused to sign a contract until a clause was inserted that forbade his roommate to eat animal crackers in bed.

In the early days of the century, players sometimes had to share a double bed when on the road. Waddell's roomie was his catcher, Ossee Schrecken-gost, who often went by the shorter last name of Schreck. The two were great pals. There was only one bone of contention between them—the chunky catcher loved to eat in bed.

Waddell began complaining to manager Connie Mack that Schreck was turning their bed into a smorgasbord. Rube was particularly vexed by his roomie's "pizzazza sandwiches." A pizzazza was made up of two slices of rye bread, thickly smeared with limburger cheese, and a layer of sliced onions in between. If the sight of the sandwich didn't make you ill, the smell sure did.

"I don't mind Ossee's pizzazzas," Rube told Mack, "but he always eats them in bed."

Mack didn't think anything of Schreck's nocturnal eating habits until the following spring, when Waddell sent his contract back unsigned. Since Rube was the team's best pitcher, the concerned manager caught the first train to Waddell's hometown in Pennsylvania for a face-to-face talk with his star lefty.

"What's the matter, Rube?" asked Mack. "Aren't you satisfied with the terms we're offering you?"

"The dough is all right, Connie," Waddell mumbled sheepishly. "But I want another clause put into it before I do any signing."

"What sort of clause?" asked the manager cautiously.

"Ossee eats those animal crackers in bed, and I don't like to sleep with all those crumbs on my sheets. Besides, his munching keeps me up at night and I lose sleep. So here's what I want. You put in my contract that Ossee Schreckengost is forbidden to eat crackers in bed."

Mack never cracked a smile. As Waddell dictated the language, the manager indulgently penned in the desired clause. Rube then signed on the dotted line of what became known forevermore as the "Animal Cracker Contract."

Super-Silly
Superstitions

◆

In no other sport are athletes as superstitious as they are in baseball. Players cling like a sweat-soaked jersey to silly quirks, weird beliefs, and wacky rituals. There is only one superstition that has always been proven to be true: It's unlucky to be behind at the end of the game. For "The Screwiest Diamond Idiosyncrasies," The Baseball Hall of SHAME inducts the following:

Mike Cuellar

Pitcher • St. Louis-Houston, N.L.; Baltimore-California, A.L. • 1964–77

Mike Cuellar was the most superstitious pitcher in major league history.

His every move on and off the diamond involved a series of strange, never-changing rituals. These formalities were his way of dealing with the gods of fate.

When the four-time 20-game winner pitched for the Baltimore Orioles, he was convinced that his rituals had given him a special, favorable rapport with Lady Luck. After each inning, he walked into the dugout, placed his glove on the "lucky end" of the bench, stopped at the water cooler for a drink, then retreated to the runway for a cigarette. He kept smoking until one Oriole hitter was retired—whether it was 30 seconds or five minutes later. Then he tossed the cigarette away, returned to the dugout, picked up his glove, and sat down in a special place on the bench. If Baltimore manager Earl Weaver inadvertently was sitting on that spot, Cuellar would make him move.

Whenever the Oriole catcher made the last out of the inning, Cuellar wouldn't budge from the bench until the catcher had put on his second shin

guard. Not the first shin guard, the second one. Only then did Cuellar go to the mound to take his warm-up pitches.

Once on the mound, he wouldn't allow anybody to throw him the ball to start his warm-up tosses. He had to pick it up off the ground, circle the mound, and walk up the mound from the second base side before he was ready to warm up.

Long aware of Cuellar's superstitious eccentricities, Cleveland Indians outfielder Alex Johnson devilishly tried to disrupt the hurler's rigid routine during a 1972 game. But Cuellar wasn't about to get whammied.

After catching a fly for the third out of the third inning, Johnson slowly carried the ball back to the infield. Timing his arrival there with Cuellar's approach to the mound, Johnson tossed the ball to the Oriole pitcher. Cuellar ducked just in time and let the ball roll free.

Helpfully, the batboy retrieved it and threw it back. Once more Cuellar squirmed from its path, and the ball dribbled toward first base. Momentarily forgetting his teammate's habits, Oriole first baseman Boog Powell threw the ball squarely at Cuellar. The pitcher caught the ball in self-defense.

Disgusted but undeterred, Cuellar—convinced the ball had been tainted—tossed it to umpire Bill Haller and asked for a new ball. The plate arbiter obliged. From his pocket Haller produced the desired replacement and threw a strike back to the mound. Again, Cuellar sidestepped nimbly. The new baseball finally trickled dead near second baseman Bobby Grich. At long last Grich showed the proper respect for his pitcher's superstitious beliefs. Gently, Grich rolled the ball to the mound. Only after it stopped did Cuellar pick it up, satisfied now that no evil spirits had invaded his place of business.

In the next inning Alex Johnson again caught a third-out fly and sought a repeat performance as he returned to the infield, ball in hand. Johnson's intended victim would have no part of it, however. Grimly, Cuellar remained in the Baltimore dugout until his Cleveland tormentor finally flipped the ball to Boog Powell. This time Powell rolled the ball to the mound. Only then did the superstitious hurler walk back onto the field—after first leaping over the top dugout step and avoiding the foul line en route to the mound.

Cuellar had a few other rituals. The night before he pitched, he always ate Chinese food. On days he was slated to pitch, he arrived in the clubhouse dressed from head to toe in blue—blue shirt, blue tie, blue suit, blue socks, and blue shoes. He also drove to the park in a blue car.

He always wore the same Orioles cap when he pitched. Once in 1975 when he was scheduled to start in Cleveland, he inadvertently left his lucky hat back in Baltimore and refused to pitch without it. So the team secretary arranged for a courier to put it on a flight to Cleveland. The hat arrived just minutes before game time.

Feeling confident now that he had his lucky hat, Cuellar threw a complete-game shutout.

Chew On This

Hall of Fame second baseman Eddie Collins had a habit of sticking a piece of chewing gum on the button of his cap as he went to bat.

Whenever he got two strikes against him, he would take the gum off his cap and chew it like crazy. One day in 1925, when Collins was player-manager of the Chicago White Sox, teammate Ted Lyons surreptitiously sprinkled red pepper on Eddie's gum after it had been placed on his cap.

When the count went to 0-and-2, Collins tore the gum off his cap and started chewing. All of a sudden he let out a whoop and spat out the gum. Then he struck out on the next pitch. Back in the dugout, he declared, "I'll fine the joker a million bucks if I ever find him."

Lou "The Mad Russian" Novikoff

Outfielder • Chicago-Philadelphia, N.L. • 1941–46

Lou "The Mad Russian" Novikoff had the weirdest superstition of any batter in baseball—he insisted that his wife Esther taunt him from the stands!

He claimed that her shouts of derision inspired him.

The superstition began when Novikoff was in the Pacific Coast League. Esther was sitting in a box seat behind home plate when he stepped up to bat. "You big bum!" she shouted. "You can't hit!" The words turned Novikoff's ears red.

He swung on the first pitch and sent the ball sailing over the left-field wall for a home run. Later, when fans asked Esther why she shouted such nasty things to her husband, she explained, "I yell at him like that to make him mad. And when he gets mad, he gets hits."

After that game Novikoff insisted that his wife continue to berate him every time he went to bat. As a result the Mad Russian won the American Association batting title and was soon called up to the Chicago Cubs. He traveled to Chicago and left his family behind in Los Angeles. But without his wife in the stands, Novikoff batted only .241 in 1941. The promising rookie looked like a flop.

The next year, the Cubs played the crosstown rival White Sox in a preseason exhibition game. When Novikoff first came to bat, Sox manager Jimmy Dykes yelled to him from the dugout, "Mad Russian, eh? If I couldn't hit any better than you, I'd be mad too."

A few days later, when Novikoff stepped into the batter's box for the season opener at Wrigley Field, a female voice rose piercingly from the box seats. "Strike the big bum out! He can't hit!" It was his loving wife Esther. Novikoff smacked a base hit, and with her in the stands almost every game, the Mad Russian went on to bat an even .300 in 1942.

When his wife's taunting didn't work, he turned to another superstition—singing. Novikoff, who had a fine baritone voice, believed that singing could change his luck. Unfortunately for those around him, he sometimes sang at the oddest times—like in the middle of the night on the train.

Once, in 1943, Novikoff got in trouble over his singing. Unable to sleep one night in Philadelphia, Cubs manager Charlie Grimm turned on the radio, which was playing music from a Philly nightclub. He bolted out of bed when he heard the master of ceremonies say, "Ladies and gentlemen, we now will hear several songs from one of our guests here tonight, Lou Novikoff, the great Cubs outfielder."

Grimm leaped into his clothes and into a taxi. He arrived at the nightclub in time to catch Novikoff's closing number. It was not a sad song from the Russian steppes. It was "My Wild Irish Rose." Grimm applauded politely and then informed Novikoff that he had just been fined for violating curfew. But the Mad Russian protested, saying he only sang that song because he thought it would bring the team good luck.

Walking the Line

New York Yankees pitcher Mel Stottlemyre never stepped on a foul line—except once.

"We were playing the Twins [in 1969] and I was headed for the bullpen to warm up before the start of the game," he recalled. "I avoided the foul line, and [Yankees coach] Jim Hegan said I shouldn't be superstitious and that I should step on the line. So I did.

"The first batter I faced was Ted Uhlaender, and he hit a line drive off my left shin. It went for a hit. Rod Carew, Tony Oliva, and Harmon Killebrew followed with extra-base hits. The fifth man hit a single and eventually scored, and I was charged with five runs. I haven't stepped on a foul line since."

New York Giants

1911

The 1911 New York Giants relied on superstitions to carry them to the National League pennant.

They believed that a player who found a stray hairpin would get a double; they avoided looking at cross-eyed girls because seeing one meant no hits; they never left more than a 25-cent tip because to do otherwise brought bad luck; they rubbed their bats with ham bones to attract hits; they wore lucky medallions, lucky ties, lucky shoes, and lucky hankies.

They also believed in their lucky mascot, a 31-year-old fan named Charley Faust.

One afternoon, early in the 1911 season, Faust sat on the bench with Giants catcher Chief Meyers and predicted the player would get a single and a double that afternoon. Meyers did. The next day Faust predicted that Meyers would get three hits. And, incredibly, Meyers did.

So Meyers went to manager John McGraw and pleaded with him to hire Faust, who then convinced the manager and the rest of the team that he would bring them good luck. So the Giants gave him a uniform and let him sit on the bench. Sure enough, the superstitious team began winning.

But midway through the season second baseman Laughing Larry Doyle fell into a batting slump. On his way to the ball park one day, he spotted a wagonload of empty beer barrels. That day he got three hits. But the next day he didn't hit the ball out of the infield.

"Maybe those barrels brought you luck," said McGraw—and a new baseball superstition was born. From then on the players believed it was good fortune to see a load of beer barrels before a ball game.

A few weeks later the Giants were in the throes of a prolonged losing streak. McGraw tried everything to snap his team out of the slump. Then he remembered his offhand comment about the barrels.

The next afternoon, as the Giants entered the Polo Grounds, a wagon loaded with beer barrels was parked near the players' entrance. Every member of the team saw the barrels, and their jubilation knew no bounds. That afternoon the Giants shook off their losing streak and won the first of eight in a row, giving them the momentum they needed to capture the pennant.

Only years later did McGraw confess that he had paid a beer-cart driver $2 to travel past his players en route to the game. The manager also revealed that after the Giants had won their eighth straight game, the driver barged into McGraw's office and demanded more money. When the manager refused, the driver stalked out—and the Giants lost that afternoon.

Billy Goat Sianis

Tavern Owner • Chicago • Oct. 6, 1945

When the Chicago Cubs refused to allow Billy Goat Sianis to bring his goat to Wrigley Field for a World Series game in 1945, he put a curse on them. According to his hex, the Cubs would never win another pennant.

In 1943 William Sianis, a tavern owner in Chicago, rescued a goat that had fallen off a truck. Sianis, a native of Greece who herded goats as a kid, kept the goat and named it Sonovia. The goat lived in a pen behind the tavern but it often wandered into the bar, where it begged swigs of booze from the patrons. Sonovia and Sianis, who was now known as Billy Goat Sianis, became inseparable.

Two years later, when the Cubs played the Detroit Tigers in the 1945 World Series, Billy Goat brought his four-legged friend to Game 4 at Wrigley Field. The Cubs had a lead of two games to one, and were only two games away from winning their first world championship since 1908.

When Billy Goat and Sonovia showed up at the Wrigley Field gate, attendants refused to let the goat into the park. Billy Goat was so incensed that he placed a hex on the team. "If Sonovia doesn't go in," he said, "the Cubs will never win another pennant. No more World Series for them."

The Cubs lost that day 4–1 and dropped two of the next three games as Detroit won the Series four games to three. It was the last time the Cubs have been in the Fall Classic.

The next time Billy Goat took a pet goat to a ball game was in 1959, when they went to Comiskey Park, home of the Chicago White Sox. Amazingly, the Sox won the pennant that year—the first time in 42 years.

In 1969, one year before his death, Billy Goat finally forgave the Cubs and lifted the hex against them. The Cubs built up a big lead by August, but then faltered badly and finished second to the New York Mets.

No one thought any more about the hex until 1973, when Sammy Goat Sianis, nephew of Billy Goat and heir to the tavern, tried to bring his goat, Socrates, with him to a game at Wrigley Field. But they were turned away at the gate. So Sammy Goat restored the hex. Within two weeks the Cubs, who had enjoyed a seven-game lead at the time, toppled from first place to second and finished the year in fifth place.

Claiming "we'd do just about anything to turn us around," Cubs chairman of the board Andrew McKenna graciously invited Sammy Goat and his pet to a game as guests of the team in 1984. Sammy Goat and his billy goat went to the game and then took off the hex. The Cubs went on to win the National League East, but lost in a playoff to the San Diego Padres. "I don't know what happened," sighed Sammy Goat. "The Cubs should have won. Maybe the hex had become too powerful. It means they need to invite me and my goat back more often to get rid of the hex."

George Stallings

Manager • Boston, N.L. • 1914

No manager had a more incredible fear of jinxes than George Stallings.

He truly believed that part of his job as skipper of the Boston Braves was to spot jinxes and ward them off. So he went to extraordinarily wacky lengths to defuse their bad influences.

Off the field, Stallings was a dignified, soft-spoken Southern gentleman, courtly of manner and meticulous in dress. But when he stepped onto the baseball diamond, he turned into a superstitious "jinx-dodger." To Stallings, even the most innocent of objects could cause his team harm.

The eccentric manager had an uncontrollable phobia over, of all things, pieces of paper. He hated them. He regarded any loose paper in front of the dugout as an omen of bad luck. The sight of a piece of paper on the floor of the Braves dugout sent him into a frenzy.

Gabe Paul, who became one of baseball's most respected general managers, used to cater to this idiosyncrasy when he was Stallings' batboy. Paul painstakingly kept the dugout area clean of any pieces of paper. "If one little scrap of paper escaped me," Paul recalled, "Mr. Stallings's roar scared the life out of me."

To thwart any ill fortune and to encourage a rally, Stallings stayed literally frozen in place whenever a Brave got a hit. Once, Stallings was bending over to pick up a peanut shell—another sign of bad luck—when a Brave socked a single. Stallings refused to move from his stooped position until the last Brave was out—which was a half hour later, because the team went wild and scored seven runs in the inning. When the rally finally ended, Stallings couldn't straighten up. Two players had to carry him back to the clubhouse, where the trainer applied hot towels to unbend him.

Stallings was constantly finding signs of bad luck and then creating ways to nullify their power. If the team's bats were crossed, he uncrossed them so his players wouldn't get hurt or go hitless that day. Sometimes he shook the bats to "wake up the lumber." He made sure his players left their gloves sitting right side up for fear they were risking an error. In close games, he slid up and down the length of the bench, hoping to pick up good luck and rub out the bad luck. Naturally, his players had to jump off the bench and make way for him when he went into his sliding mode.

Stallings seldom saw outfielder Josh Devore catch a ball. Devore, who was traded to Boston late in the year, had cement hands. One day, late in a tie game, a high fly was hit to him in right field. Devore circled under the ball with uncertainty. The tension over whether or not he would catch it was too much for Stallings to bear. The manager leaped from the bench and rushed to the clubhouse door. He stood with his back to the diamond for half a minute before he turned and asked in a voice hoarse with anxiety, "Did he catch it?" Devore did. After that, whenever there was a high fly hit to Devore, Stallings turned his back on him.

The manager's obsession with jinxes had a bizarre effect on the Braves. The team, which had only one .300 hitter and an error-prone outfield, was wallowing in the National League cellar 11 games behind the New York Giants in mid-July, 1914. But then Stallings convinced most of the players they could not lose because he was using counteracting whammies on all jinxes. Incredibly, the Braves started winning, and, in the most amazing turn-around in baseball history, went on to capture not only the pennant, but the World Series.

Stallings never did win another pennant, despite his best jinx-dodging efforts. Still, the superstitious manager stuck with his wacky beliefs and expected his players to follow suit.

In 1918, when the club lost nine straight games and sat through seven straight rainouts, Stallings searched for the jinx that was victimizing his team. Suddenly it dawned on him. His catcher, John Henry, was sporting a dandy mustache that he had grown about the time the Braves' troubles started. So Stallings ordered Henry to shave off the mustache. When the player balked, Stallings threatened to release him that very day. Henry shaved it off . . . and the Braves won that afternoon.

Shamefully Weird Superstitions

Dion James, Atlanta Braves—In 1988, during the outfielder's 16-game hitting streak, he refused to wash his underwear. "People didn't like to get close to me," he said.

Kevin Elster, New York Mets—Once, during the 1988 season, Elster took his bat to bed, and the next day he walloped a homer. So that night he took his bat to bed again, and even invited his bat to lunch the next day. "The bat picked up the check," said Elster, who later that night smacked another homer.

Tito Fuentes, San Francisco Giants—Throughout his playing career with the team (1965–74), he allegedly sprayed "voodoo juice" on his glove, arms, hands, and feet. Then he stuffed into his back pocket a special packet containing an eagle's claw and turtle shells.

Pepe Frias, Montreal Expos—Frias, who played throughout the 1970s, would grab the leg of any teammate who sat next to him in the dugout whenever an Expo was running the bases. When asked why he did this, Frias explained, "This makes the man on base run faster."

Vida Blue, Oakland Athletics—Blue believed that the same baseball hat he had worn since Opening Day 1974 brought him good luck for three straight seasons. But in 1977 the umpires refused to let him wear it because it was faded and soiled. When Blue persisted, he was threatened with a fine and ejection. He finally conceded, but not before he ceremoniously burned the hat on the field before a game. He then proceeded to lose a league-high 19 games that year.

Bobo Newsom—The most traveled hurler in major league history would never tie his own shoelaces on the day he was scheduled to pitch. He'd suit up and stand in the middle of the clubhouse until somebody came over, knelt down, and laced his shoes.

Bill McKechnie, Cincinnati Reds—The manager and his players believed they won the pennant in 1940 because of an old dirty tie he owned. He wore the magic tie day in and day out, and sometimes slept with it because, he claimed, it had special powers that would pull the team through tight spots.

Babe Ruth, New York Yankees—Babe would never lend one of his bats to a teammate. Explained Ruth, "Bats have so many hits in them, and each time I lend one to a guy and he whacks out a couple of hits, all I'm doing is lopping a few points off Babe Ruth's batting average. That's why nobody uses Babe Ruth's bat—but Babe Ruth!"

GOING, GOING, GONE!

◆

Along with the RBI and ERA, baseball should include such statistics as AWOL and CVC (Curfew Violators Caught). Some players would rather play hooky than baseball. They've been known to skip out on the team for a day or even a week. Others believe that curfews are only for teenagers with strict parents. For "The Most Notorious AWOLs and Curfew Violators," The Baseball Hall of SHAME inducts the following:

Rollie Hemsley

Catcher • Pittsburgh-Chicago-Cincinnati-Philadelphia, St. Louis, N.L.; St. Louis-Cleveland-New York, A.L. • 1928–47

Rollie Hemsley played his best during those hours when all good players were in bed.

He caught fastballs during the day and hell during the night. Throughout the 1930s and '40s, Rollicking Rollie led the league in fines and suspensions. The new marks he established in late-night carousing and fights were often black eyes and split lips.

His uproarious off-the-field life gave Cleveland Indians skipper Oscar Vitt such fits that the team paid Hemsley's wife a salary plus expenses to keep a leash on him. Her job was to wait outside the clubhouse door after each game, nab Rollie as he came out, and deliver him to Vitt in good condition by noon the next day.

"I guess I was worse than Peck's bad boy," Hemsley admitted years later, after he cleaned up his act for good.

Before he reformed, Rollicking Rollie lived by the credo, "Eat, drink, and be merry, for tomorrow we play a double-header." He loved to party and he loved to play. Once, after an errant throw hit Hemsley in the head and left him woozy, the team trainer wanted to take him out of the game. "Naw," said Hemsley. "I've started games dizzier than this."

UPI/Bettmann Newsphotos

He didn't have career years, he had career *nights*. He once wound up in three jails in three different New York boroughs in one night. In another classic moment, he walked into a hotel lobby with a bottle of whiskey in one hand and a bottle of seltzer water in the other. He asked three dignified old ladies to join him in a drink, and when they refused, he sprayed them with seltzer.

Because of his escapades, Hemsley was passed around the majors like an old rumor. He played on seven clubs, and despite his late-hour larks had a talent for handling young pitchers. He also had a .262 lifetime batting average, which was hardly cause for shame.

But his revelries were—especially when he was with the St. Louis Browns. In his four-year stint there from 1934–37, Rollie racked up $5,000 in fines levied by strait-laced manager Roger Hornsby. Hemsley's most infamous fine in 1936 involved, of all things, frogs, shoes, and knitting.

On the train from Detroit to Washington, Hemsley brought a large wicker basket full of live frogs. Late at night Hemsley planted three-dozen croakers in the berths of his teammates. Even Hornsby, his manager, got a few of them. Naturally, pandemonium broke loose.

The next day Hornsby warned Hemsley to cut the buffoonery. But as soon as the Browns were on the train again, Rollie was up to his midnight madness. In the wee hours he collected all his teammates' shoes from beneath their berths. Then he tied the shoes together and hid them. The next morning Hemsley walked off the Pullman, while his teammates, assisted by railroad officials, made a frantic search for their shoes. This brought another warning for the bad boy of the Browns.

A week later Hemsley, determined to show his contempt for Hornsby's rigid rules, sat in the train's smoking compartment knitting with a ball of yarn and two needles. "This is about all a guy can do on this ball club without being hauled over the coals," he announced to the press.

A few hours later he convinced a couple of teammates to march lockstep style in front of Hornsby's drawing room. That did it. The manager slapped Hemsley with a $300 fine.

Rollie simply couldn't be trusted. The night before a double-header with the Yankees in 1935, Hemsley learned that he was the lone available catcher for the Browns because of injuries to the other receivers.

Hornsby had a heart-to-heart talk with Hemsley in the hotel lobby. "Now listen, Rollie," said the manager. "You have to work the double-header. I want you to promise me that you'll make good on this assignment. Cut out your foolish stuff for one night, please. Get to bed early, because if you're in shape tomorrow, we can knock off those Yankees."

Hemsley sealed the bargain with a hearty handshake. "You can rely on me, Rog."

Sending a bed-checker around to Hemsley's room at 11 P.M., Hornsby was told that Rollie was sound asleep. But Hemsley was not to be found an hour later—or ten hours later. He had disappeared into the night and didn't stagger back until 10 A.M., sporting two shiners and a massive hangover. "That'll cost you 250 dollars," barked Hornsby, who then ordered Rollie to sit in a tub of ice. "I don't care how badly you feel, you're catching both games."

So with one eye nearly swollen shut and the other half closed, Hemsley caught the double-header. "Boy, did I suffer out there," he recalled. "It was murder."

A hail-fellow-well-met, Rollie couldn't stay away from where the action was. Whenever he felt he was Jack Dempsey, someone else took on the role of Joe Louis. The results were two shiners for Hemsley. "I had so many black eyes," he once said, "that some of my friends thought I was born with them."

In Philadelphia in 1934, he engaged in an altercation with a policeman. Rollie came out the winner in the fistic battle, gaining possession of the cop's nightstick, shield, and revolver. But he was arrested for the victory. Hornsby bailed him out and then suspended him. Another time, Rollie found a group of sailors in a bitter debate on a street corner in Boston. Hemsley tried to play the role of peacemaker but was told to get lost. Before he obeyed, he chalked up decisions over half the sailors.

In 1932 when Rollie was with the Chicago Cubs, manager Charlie Grimm had to crawl from a warm bed at 3 A.M. to rescue him from five policemen who were dragging him away.

Not every night was a hellbender. One of his favorite stunts was to impersonate a waiter or bartender. One night a group of baseball writers ordered drinks in the hotel lobby. In walked Hemsley, dressed in a white jacket and balancing a tray. He served the drinks with finesse, solemnly watched as the check was signed, pocketed the quarter tip, and bowed his way out.

One time, at the team's hotel, Hemsley told the bellhops, "You fellows aren't getting half enough tips. I'll show you how." He lugged baggage, delivered ice, and showed guests their rooms. At the crack of dawn Hemsley turned over his night's receipts, which, according to the hotel, shattered all local records.

In 1938, when Hornsby couldn't take any more of Hemsley's after-hour shenanigans, Rollie was traded to the Cleveland Indians. Spring training wasn't even two weeks old before Hemsley had been fined once and suspended another time for late-night carousing. After he was caught breaking training rules for the third time in his first ten days as an Indian, Rollie was sent home until he promised to mend his wild ways. He promised to be good, but he failed to keep his word.

Fans from across the country sent manager Oscar Vitt letters on how to handle Hemsley. "I received a thousand suggestions," said Vitt. "Cures, mystic rings, places to send him. One guy wrote that he was a baseball nut and would guard Hemsley day and night if I'd let him join the club."

Nothing worked. One night, while the team's train was heading for New York, Rollie stayed up all night and wreaked havoc on the Pullman. He kicked spittoons up and down the aisles, tossed lighted matches into unoccupied upper berths, doused sleeping passengers with water, and crooned lustily—off-key. For a finale he climbed into the berth where Vitt was sleeping. Vitt suspended the playful catcher and ordered him to return to Cleveland.

That was Rollie's last blast. Just when everyone was ready to give up on him, he suddenly turned his life around and walked a path as straight and narrow as a foul line.

Guilty Consciences

During spring training in 1965, Washington Senators manager Gil Hodges spotted four of his players sneaking out of the team hotel past curfew.

The next day at a clubhouse meeting he announced, "I know there were four guys out past the curfew last night. I saw you. I won't embarrass you by naming names, but you know who you are. You're each fined 50 dollars. So give your check to [coach] Joe Pignatano today. If I have to come to you tomorrow and ask for your fine, it'll cost you 100 dollars."

Later that day Pignatano told Hodges, "You know those four guys you fined this morning? Well, seven of them have paid the fine already."

Jesse Barnes

Pitcher • New York, N.L. • 1922

Jesse Barnes was perhaps the only curfew violator in baseball who made money because he *did* get nabbed for breaking the rules.

Barnes, then one of the New York Giants' best pitchers, just never could see why anyone should be in bed by midnight. So most every chance he got, he sneaked out for some late-night fun. More often than not, he made it back without anyone being the wiser. But occasionally he was nailed and fined by manager John McGraw.

During the 1922 season, McGraw caught Barnes sneaking back to his room after curfew and fined him $100. "Next time I catch you, it'll be 200 dollars," snapped the manager.

A few weeks later in Philadelphia, Barnes partied until the wee hours of the morning. Rather than risk going through the lobby of the team's hotel, Barnes tried climbing up the fire escape to his room. But he slipped and fell on one of the iron rungs and badly bruised his shins.

Later that morning he walked into the clubhouse with a noticeable limp. McGraw stared at Barnes coldly and asked, "What happened to you?"

Barnes screwed up his face in pain and hobbled toward his locker. "I slipped on a cake of soap in the bathtub."

The answer was too glib to fool an old campaigner like the Little Napoleon. "Slipped on a cake of soap, huh? Well, that's pretty dumb. You're fined 200 dollars—and next time, don't use any soap."

The next day the newspapers ran the story of Barnes's fine and his lame excuse. One of the executives of a company that made rubber bath mats read the story and got a brainstorm. He called up Barnes and offered to pay him $1,000 for a testimonial. Barnes agreed in a flash.

Within a week an ad appeared in the papers showing a photo of the smiling pitcher with one leg over the tub. Underneath, the caption read, "If Jesse Barnes had used NONSKID BATH MATS, he wouldn't have slipped in his tub."

Thanks to his little indiscretion, Barnes walked, or rather limped, away with a tidy $800 profit.

Win a Bet; Lose a Friend

From 1903 to 1907 Ossee Schreckengost was more than just a catcher for the Philadelphia A's. He was also a "big brother" to the team's talented but wayward pitcher, Rube Waddell.

One morning Waddell woke up in a hospital bruised and suffering from a slight concussion. He told Ossee, "The last thing I remember was having a few drinks in our hotel room. What happened?"

"You decided you could fly and went out the window," Ossee replied matter-of-factly.

Waddell sat up in his bed. "I could have been killed! Why didn't you stop me?"

"What?" said Ossee. "And lose the hundred bucks I bet that you could do it?"

Jumping Joe Dugan

Third Baseman • Philadelphia-Boston-New York-Detroit, A.L.; Boston, N.L. • 1917–1931

Jumping Joe Dugan earned his nickname for one reason. Early in his career he was always jumping the club—because he was homesick.

Dugan went scooting home to his mother so often—about every few weeks—that manager Connie Mack wouldn't pencil him in the lineup until seeing firsthand that Dugan had arrived in the clubhouse.

Drafted by the Philadelphia Athletics after his freshman year in college, the 19-year-old rookie had a difficult time adjusting to life in the bigs. And cold-hearted Philly fans only made it worse for him.

Struggling at the plate with a batting average below .200, Dugan was stung by the viciousness of the fans. "When they jeer, there's nothing harder to bear," wrote a local sportswriter at the time. It didn't take the fans long to discover that the rookie infielder was a sensitive college boy. They took no pity. They rode him unmercifully.

Dugan first packed his bags and ran home to Mother after striking out twice with men on base in a game against the Yankees. On his way out the clubhouse door Dugan told the press he was "heartbroken" and "through as a major leaguer." But after a few days with Mom in New Haven, Connecticut, and long-distance pleas from Connie Mack, Dugan returned.

This soon became a pattern: a bad game, boos ringing in his ears, and an unscheduled trip to Mom. Sometimes Dugan returned in time to play the next game and sometimes he didn't. Since the Athletics were perennial cellar dwellers anyway, Dugan didn't think his absences mattered. Besides, he said

at the time, it was more important for him to be with his mother when she needed him. Or when he needed her.

Philly fans were not so understanding. Every time he came up to bat, they'd shout, "Run home to Mama!" or "I wanna go home!" or "Why don't you stay home and let your mother bat for you!"

The fans, who earlier in the decade had cheered for local hero "Home Run" Baker, began calling Joe "Run Home" Dugan. But it was *Philadelphia Inquirer* sportswriter Tony Maxwell who coined the moniker that stuck for the rest of Dugan's life—"Jumping Joe."

"It was tough," Dugan recalled years later. "I didn't belong in the majors at that age. I should have spent time in the minors, but it was a war year and they needed players.

"I never liked Philadelphia. I just couldn't get used to the town, and I tried mighty hard, because I liked to play ball and I was very fond of Connie Mack. But I could stand it just so long."

Although Dugan eventually got over his homesickness and learned how to hit, he remained a habitual AWOL during his five-year stint with the Athletics. When he was in the mood to see a new Broadway show, he simply jumped the club and took the train to New York. When the urge struck him to visit with old college pals, he headed off for Boston.

Dugan wanted Connie Mack to trade him so he could leave Philadelphia for good, but the manager refused to even consider it until late in the 1921 season after Dugan pulled another unscheduled leave of absence.

"Connie was more like a dad than a manager, and I'm afraid I abused his sympathetic attitude," recalled Dugan. "One day I decided that a little surf bathing would be more exhilarating to the Dugan constitution than combat with the Red Sox, so I shoved off for Atlantic City. I had a very enjoyable sojourn. When I returned, Connie said to me, 'I am going to try to figure how I can get along without you next season. Somehow, I don't think it's going to be very difficult.'"

The following year Dugan was traded to the Boston Red Sox and then to the Yankees, where he developed into one of the league's best third basemen. Although he finally lived up to his potential and matured, Dugan never could shake the handle of "Jumping Joe."

Shameful Moments for AWOLs

1988—White Sox outfielder Ivan Calderon was supposed to pinch-hit when the Sox loaded the bases in a game against the Kansas City Royals. But manager Jim Fregosi couldn't find him, so another batter was sent up and popped out. Where was Calderon? In the clubhouse—watching videotapes of himself hitting.

1988—On the first pitch of a game against the Milwaukee Brewers, the California Angels had only eight men on the field. That's because Angels center fielder Devon White was still in the clubhouse talking on the telephone! The pitch, a strike to Jim Gantner, was nullified by the umpires. When the game was restarted, with White now in center field, Gantner rapped a single.

1987—Chicago Cubs catcher Jody Davis became the first player benched for filming a TV spot. Taping ran long and Davis was late for batting practice, so angry manager Gene Michael sat him down.

1959—The Washington Senators rookie shortstop Zoilo Versalles disappeared from training camp for three days. But he hadn't really jumped the team. The Cuban-born rookie had gone to manager Cookie Lavagetto and told him that he had no change of clothes because he had hocked his wardrobe. He asked for a cash advance to bail out his clothes.

Lavagetto gave him the money. "But," recalled the manager, "how was I to know that the hock shop was in Havana?"

Bugs Raymond

Pitcher • Detroit, A.L.; St. Louis-New York, N.L. • 1904–11

More than any other player, pitcher Bugs Raymond was responsible for the bane of all curfew breakers—bed checks and team-hired detectives.

Bugs was the major league's all-time elbow-bender—a nocturnal party animal who foraged in nightspots and cabarets looking for a good time. He never failed to find it either. The problem was that when he painted the town red, it often took him all night, sometimes even days, to do it.

A free spirit, Bugs was closing up a Manhattan nightclub when a waiter asked him how he threw his spitball. Bugs got up, gripped a water glass, and said, "Well, I wet these two fingers, throw my leg up, and go like this." He then threw the glass tumbler through a window. "Note," he said with a straight face, "the break."

Because of Bugs's notoriety, teams feared other players would follow his example. Soon more clubs than ever had coaches doing bed checks and detectives trailing night owls.

Dumped by two teams that couldn't control his wee-hour sprees, Bugs wound up with the New York Giants in 1909. In his first season with the Giants he won 18 games, and manager John McGraw was hailed as the handler par excellence of the unmanageable.

One of the first things McGraw did was hire a private eye to tail Bugs on his first night as a Giant. The next day the detective gave the manager a detailed report on Raymond's rounds at Harlem nighteries. McGraw then handed the report to Bugs when the pitcher walked bleary-eyed into the clubhouse.

Bugs studied the report, which said he had consumed beers, ryes, cheese, crackers, pretzels, and with each libation, several onions. "That's a lie!" Bugs roared. "I hate onions and never had none!"

So McGraw decided that instead of a detective he would hire a bodyguard whose sole job was to keep Bugs Raymond out of trouble. Never one to stand on ceremony, Bugs quickly befriended the guard assigned to watch him, a man named Fuller. As the two toured the saloons, Bugs gleefully announced, "This is my keeper. I'm full, but he's Fuller."

When Bugs and his bodyguard failed to show up at the ball park the next afternoon, McGraw sent a detective to find them. They were located two blocks from the Polo Grounds, in a bar where the duo were still engaged in a drinking contest.

McGraw suspended Bugs. The next day the pitcher was in his Giants uniform—tending bar in his favorite saloon.

In retaliation McGraw tried to curb Bugs's late-night fun by sending the pitcher's salary directly to his wife. The manager figured that if Bugs had no funds, he would not prowl the wild side of the street.

McGraw let Bugs have some spending money to get by. But when Bugs asked McGraw for an advance, the manager refused, claiming Bugs would blow it on a good time. So Bugs came up with a scheme to counter the shortfall of funds. He told McGraw he needed money to buy underwear and shirts. Rather than give Bugs the money which McGraw knew would wind up in a taproom till, the wily manager tried to outfox him. McGraw sent him to a haberdashery on Broadway in the care of coach Jesse Burkett. Bugs purchased $25 worth of goods and his keeper paid the bill. But then, two hours later, Bugs went back to the store and told the clerk that his wife did not like anything he had bought. "Give me back the 25 dollars and she will be around tomorrow to buy what she likes," he said. The clerk complied. With the $25, Bugs went off on one of the wildest binges of his career.

He wasn't seen for three days. Burkett finally found him at a marathon party and told him, "McGraw needs you badly, and he told me to tell you it's your turn to pitch today."

"Nothing doing," said Bugs.

"What do you mean by nothing doing?"

"Just this: Since McGraw is sending my salary to my wife, let her pitch for him."

McGraw next tried bribery. He offered Bugs a bonus and a raise if only he would straighten up and fly right. Bugs said he was willing to try. But soon it became a game to see if he could sneak a drink for the fun of it.

It wasn't unusual for him to slip out of the bullpen during the game, sell a ball for 50 cents, and, with the proceeds, dash across the street to a bar for a cold brew. But eventually he got caught.

The next time, when McGraw needed him to pitch the second game of a double-header, Bugs was told to stay in the clubhouse, where guards kept an eye on the doors so he couldn't sneak out. Undaunted, Bugs lowered an empty bucket out of the clubhouse window and a confederate filled it with beer.

Because of Bugs's reputation, gamblers thought they could cash in on his fondness for barhopping. A group of high rollers plotted to get him drunk enough so he'd lose a game against the Chicago Cubs, on whom they had bet a big bundle.

The gamblers befriended Bugs, who quickly figured out their scheme. So he took them to his favorite watering hole and gave the bartender a wink. A gin bottle was placed on the bar and Bugs started drinking from it while the others quaffed beer.

After he had consumed half the bottle, Bugs said, "Fellows, I've got to break away. I'm pitching this afternoon." With that, he poured the rest of the bottle into a tumbler, swallowed it with one gulp, and staggered out.

Bugs then went out and tossed a shutout. He wasn't drunk at all. That's because the bottle labeled "gin" contained nothing but water.

WHO ELSE BELONGS IN THE BASEBALL HALL OF SHAME?

◆

Do you have any nominations for The Baseball Hall of SHAME? Give us your picks for the most shameful, funny, embarrassing, wacky, boneheaded moments in baseball history. Here's your opportunity to pay a lighthearted tribute to the game we all love.

Please describe your nominations in detail. Those nominations that are documented with the greatest number of facts, such as firsthand accounts, newspaper or magazine clippings, box scores, or photos, have the best chance of being inducted into The Baseball Hall of SHAME. Feel free to send as many nominations as you wish. If you don't find an existing category listed in our Baseball Hall of SHAME books that fits your nomination, then make up your own category. All submitted material becomes the property of The Baseball Hall of SHAME and is nonreturnable. Mail your nominations to:

The Baseball Hall of SHAME
P.O. Box 31867
Palm Beach Gardens, FL 33420